bild

Understanding Support Services for People with Learning Disabilities

Alice Bradley

Supporting the Learning Disability Awards Framework

Higher Professional Diploma (Level 4)

Unit 1: Understanding Learning Disability Services

British Library Cataloguing in Publication Data

A CIP record for this book is available from the Public Library

© BILD Publications 2005

BILD Publications is the imprint of:
British Institute of Learning Disabilities
Campion House
Green Street
Kidderminster
Worcestershire DY10 1JL

Telephone: 01562 723010
Fax: 01562 723029
E-mail: enquiries@bild.org.uk

Website: www.bild.org.uk

ISBN 1 904082 94 7

BILD publications are distributed by:
BookSource
32 Finlas Street
Cowlairs Estate
Glasgow G22 5DU

Telephone: 08702 402182
Fax: 0141 5770189

For a publications catalogue with details of all BILD books and journals telephone 01562 723010, e-mail enquiries@bild.org.uk or visit the BILD website: www.bild.org.uk

About the British Institute of Learning Disabilities

The British Institute of Learning Disabilities is committed to improving the quality of life for people with a learning disability by involving them and their families in all aspects of our work, working with government and public bodies to achieve full citizenship, undertaking beneficial research and development projects and helping service providers to develop and share good practice.

Acknowledgements

I'd like to thank everyone who assisted me with this book by sharing their ideas, opinions and experiences with me. Special thanks to the people of the Advisory and Support Group and to staff at BILD for their usual high level of support.

About the author

Alice Bradley is a freelance trainer and consultant and an Open University tutor. She has worked with people with learning disabilities of all ages, as well as families and professionals, for many years in schools, urban and rural communities and higher education establishments in the UK and several countries in Asia and Africa. She is currently undertaking work for BILD, the Scottish Consortium for Learning Disability and the Scottish Qualifications Authority. She is the author of many books on learning disabilities.

Contents

		Page
	Introduction	9
Chapter 1	The history of learning disability	13
Chapter 2	The concept of learning disability	31
Chapter 3	The current context of support services	49
Chapter 4	Person centred planning	65
Chapter 5	Models of disability and their effects on service development	79
Chapter 6	Networking	89
	References	99
	Resources	103

Introduction

This book is intended for managers and senior practitioners concerned with support services for people with learning disabilities who want to continue their professional development. It should also be of interest to senior staff and managers who are preparing for the Learning Disabilities Awards Framework (LDAF) Higher Professional Diploma (Level 4) Unit 1: Understanding Learning Disability Services and studying S/NVQ at Level 4.

The purpose of the book is to:

- highlight issues relevant to managers and senior practitioners with particular emphasis upon the effects of history on support services for people with learning disabilities, the concept of 'learning disability' and its implications for support services, person centred approaches to services, social inclusion and the rights of people with learning disabilities

- draw upon relevant research studies as the basis for deeper understanding of the issues explored

- encourage reflection and subsequent action

- raise issues which should stimulate further discussion and possibly research

- provide information about useful organisations and publications

How the book is organised

The book has six chapters:

Chapter 1	The history of learning disabilities, reviews the historical context of services and the effects of negative perceptions of people with learning disabilities on service provision.
Chapter 2	The concept of learning disability, is about current understanding of the term 'learning disability', the dilemmas this causes and the possible effects of learning disability on people's lives.
Chapter 3	The current context of support services, explores the context within which services currently operate, with particular reference to empowerment, advocacy and social inclusion.
Chapter 4	Person centred planning, is about approaches which enable people to be in control of their own lives.
Chapter 5	Models of disability and their effects on service development, is an analysis of different ways of understanding disability. In particular, the medical and social models of disability are discussed and compared.
Chapter 6	Networking, focuses on the importance of a range of partnerships and alliances for the benefits of the people supported by a service.

Following Chapter 6 there are references and a resources section that includes useful contact addresses and suggestions for additional reading.

The LDAF Higher Professional Diploma (Level 4)

The Higher Professional Diploma is intended for senior workers in roles associated with services supporting adults with learning disabilities, eg supported employment or supported living, residential or respite services, day care and community based support services. There are two pathways to the diploma – Managing Learning Disability Services and Senior Practitioner in Learning Disability Services – each requiring a particular combination of units from the unit bank. Learners need to complete twelve units to achieve the full qualification. Further information is available at www.city-and-guilds.co.uk

Understanding Learning Disability Services, the unit addressed in this book, is a mandatory unit for both pathways. All of the topics required for successful completion of this unit are covered in this book. The aims and outcomes of this LDAF unit are listed below.

Aims

This unit aims to enable the learner to:

- explore what learning disability is and the impact of different models for defining it

- consider the historical context of services for people with learning disabilities

- investigate the concept of person centred planning and its impact on service design and delivery

- consider the importance of networks to a learning disability service

Outcomes

On successful completion of this unit the learner will be able to:

- understand the concept of 'learning disability'

- reflect on the historical context of learning disability services

- understand the current context of learning disability services

- review the structures and systems which support person centred planning

- analyse how different models of disability affect service development

- discuss the importance of a learning disability service using regional networks

Non-diploma readers

For readers not undertaking the LDAF diploma the book serves as a stand-alone text which contributes to Continuing Professional Development (CPD) or a qualification other than LDAF.

Activities and reflections

Learning is only as good as the use we put it to – in this instance, its impact upon practice. There are likely to be topics in this book with which you are already very familiar. A particular slant might cause you to think about these in different ways. There will be other areas less familiar to you. To capitalise on opportunities for interaction with the text there are, at intervals throughout the book, activities and reflections which encourage you to consider how the particular issue under discussion relates to your own situation and experience. These interactions also help you prepare for your assignment if you are a LDAF candidate. In addition, you might find them useful as the basis for discussion at staff meetings or for staff supervision purposes.

The advisory and support group

Several people assisted with this book by sharing their opinions and experiences. These were the advisory and support group which consists of people with learning disabilities, family carers, support staff and managers who made the issues come alive. Above all, they have first-hand experience of support services, as providers or service users, obtained over a number of years which have seen considerable changes in understanding, approaches and developments in service provision. With their insights and support, and those of people like them, we can perhaps move forward together towards better futures for the people services support.

Chapter 1

The history of learning disability

Introduction

The social, economic, political and technological world we live in is substantially different from that of yesterday. In many ways the changes experienced by people with learning disabilities have been more substantial than for most others. Today's constantly recurring themes – rights, empowerment, inclusion, self-advocacy, participation and so on – are very different from those of even thirty or forty years ago. History is a good teacher, but only if we are prepared to learn the right lessons.

This first chapter takes a brief look back at some of the significant events of learning disability history and highlights particularly the effect of negative perceptions of people with learning disabilities in the past and the way in which these shaped the development of services at particular points in history. But it is also about the persistent effect some of these negative attitudes exert today. The aim in this chapter is to:

- undertake a brief review of the major historical influences on the lives of people with learning disabilities since the late nineteenth century

- explore the ways in which these have affected the provision and development of support services for people with learning disabilities and their families

History and learning disability

Clark (1986, in Gates and Wilberforce, 2003) writes, 'Learning disability has been a source of speculation, fear and scientific enquiry for hundreds of years. It has been regarded in turn as an administrative, medical, eugenic, educational and social problem' (p.8).

It is generally considered that the industrial revolution, with its increasing mechanisation, population growth and division of labour had profound social implications for people with learning disabilities, as well as for others considered unproductive within society. One outcome was a steady growth in the number of public institutions designed to house those who didn't conform to the changing economic, social and political climate (Brigham, 2000). At the same time, religious ideas, which had been the basis of humane, if paternalistic, services, were gradually being replaced by a belief in the power of science. Eugenics – the preservation of the 'purity' of the human race through selective breeding – gained credence both in the UK and internationally. Francis Galton, who coined the term eugenics in 1883, 'advocated two forms of eugenics: one was to promote procreation in the intellectual classes, a process termed *positive eugenics*, whilst the other was inhibition of procreation amongst classes that were considered to be socially deviant, a process termed *negative eugenics*.' People with learning disabilities were perceived as social deviants with a tendency to propagate 'their own kind' and thus lead to the degeneration of society 'through the erosion of its physical, intellectual and moral qualities' (Atherton, 2003, p.47).

Although institutions had existed for some time prior to these events, official backing for their expansion – and their regimes of social control – was made more explicit through new legislation, which included:

- the 1908 Report of the Royal Commission on Care and Control of the Feeble-Minded (1904–08) which 'concluded that those individuals suffering from feeble-mindedness and the associated conditions of insanity, epilepsy, alcoholism, criminality and pauperism were a threat to the stability of society' (Tredgold, 1909 in Atherton, 2003) and recommended state intervention in the form of institutionalisation

- the 1912 Bill and 1913 Mental Deficiency Act, which identified four categories of mental defect – *idiot, imbecile, feeble-minded* and *moral defectives* – and provided the basis for certification; persons who were thus certified were to be 'sent or placed into an institution for defectives or placed under guardianship'

- the 1927 Mental Deficiency (Amendment) Act

- the 1929 Report of the Wood Committee which introduced the terms *mental defective* and *mental deficiency* and advocated the development of 'colonies' where people would spend their whole lives and contact with the outside world be minimised

(Atkinson et al, 1997; Atherton, 2003)

Institutions started to become more common in the early 1800s and initially housed people with learning disabilities and those with mental health difficulties, as well as others considered vulnerable. Many were founded initially on humanitarian principles and stressed the educability of people described as 'feeble-minded'. For example, the pioneering educationalist Edouard Seguin (1837 on) established a number of schools for people with learning disabilities which were intended as 'sanctuaries from an uncaring world' (Brigham, 2000, p.34). Residents were seen as innocents, uncorrupted by the concerns of the outside world (a notion that gave rise to the idea of the person with a learning disability as an 'eternal child', something that persists to this day, as evidenced by the many media reports that describe adults with learning disabilities in terms of their so-called 'mental age'). Emphasis in these establishments was on teaching people simple skills so that they could return to their own communities.

However, in the early part of the 20th century, not least because of the influence of the eugenics movement, institutions became much more custodial and a means of segregating and controlling people. Admission to an institution could be at the request of the family, or the result of a petition from a number of people, sanctioned by the signatures of two doctors. As mentioned above, the 1913 Mental Deficiency Act provided a means of certifying people into one of four categories. The tendency to classify people with a learning disability persists to this day.

Potts (2000) describes the classification of human beings as an attempt to 'construct a hermetic seal between "normal" and "subnormal" people, led in England, by medical practitioners whose aim was to control the spread of social disease' (p.44). She identifies several factors which advanced the development of institutions for 'separated' people: the costs of providing for unemployed, sick or destitute people before the advent of the welfare state, the influence of the emerging medical profession, the difficulties of working class people in expanding industrialised cities, the distinction between 'criminals' and 'paupers', and 'lunatics' and 'idiots', and the development of psychometric testing. She cites three approaches to classification which were particularly influential at the time:

- the work of Dr John Langdon-Down who used the analogy of race and identified 'mongolism' as a more primitive evolutionary stage

- the work of Dr A. F. Tredgold who was Medical Expert to the Royal Commission on the Care and Control of the Feeble-Minded (1904–08) which led to legislation on compulsory detention; he classified human beings into two groups, 'normal' and 'defective', and wrote extensively for the Eugenics Review

- *The Fundamentals of School Health* by Dr James Kerr (1926) in which different levels of intelligence are categorised by the use of Intelligence Quotients (IQs), 'reflecting the growing influence of psychology in the assessment of learning capacities' (p.49)

Potts illustrates how the physical environment of the institutions reflected changes in ideology over time. She compares Earlswood, built in 1845, in which Langdon-Down 'built up a reputation for enlightened treatment' (p.53) based on his belief that people with learning disabilities should and could be educated, and St Lawrence's, opened in 1870, where the physical surroundings are penitential. Whereas Earlswood was built for around four hundred people, St Lawrence's accommodated over a thousand and was 'a world apart and accommodated a shift in political and professional attitudes away from "alleviation" towards compulsory detention and sterilisation' (p.55).

Fido and Potts (1997) write: 'Life-long institutionalisation for most, if not all, 'mental defectives' both for 'their own protection and the protection of others' became an energetic crusade. The Mental Deficiency Act of 1913, the first truly effective legislation in this field, was meant to 'protect and provide asylum for the most vulnerable people in society' (Styring, 2003, p.113) but resulted in the incarceration of large numbers of people. Under this Act, local authorities were required to certify all 'mental defectives' and to set up special certified institutions. The 1913 Act was not fully implemented for some time, because of the First World War, but the report of the Wood Committee in 1929 resulted in an acceleration of the institutionalisation of people with learning disabilities.

Walmsley's (1997) investigation of archive sources from the Bedfordshire County Record Office illustrates the use of the 1913 Act in that county. One example in 1915 is of twenty-one-year-old Dora Ann S. who had been found 'wandering and with no visible means of support' and who was described by the Deputy County Medical Officer of Health as: 'a menace to the troops as she had been sleeping with various soldiers in the neighbourhood and complaints had been made by the military to the police of the girl's conduct'. She was described in the report as 'healthy but somewhat dull' and without 'sufficient mental control to resist men who wish to assault her' (p.98). She had shown no 'immoral tendencies' until she had been assaulted when in domestic service, 'but from that time until the present she appears to have been immoral whenever opportunity has occurred'.

Dora was sent to an institution for 'fallen girls' in London. Her mother had to testify that her 'defect' had been present from an early age, one of the requirements for certification. Walmsley highlights the fact that blame was attributed to Dora, rather than the men who approached her or her stepfather whom she had accused of molesting her, a common response of the time which epitomised the concern about 'feeble-minded' women and their sexuality as a threat to the purity of the race (Brigham, 2000).

People who remained at home did not avoid the reaches of the Act. In the same account, Walmsley describes how the families of children with learning disabilities, and people with learning disabilities, living in the county were subjected to regular scrutiny of all aspects of their lives, even the most intimate, by 'voluntary visitors' from the Bedfordshire Voluntary Association for the Care of the Mentally Defective, and judgemental reports made on these supervisory visits.

You might like to read . . .

'Uncovering Community Care: Evidence in a County Record Office' by Jan Walmsley in Atkinson et al (eds) (1997) *Forgotten Lives: Exploring the History of Learning Disability* Kidderminster, BILD

'Understanding segregation from the nineteenth to the twentieth century: redrawing boundaries and the problems of pollution' by Lindsay Brigham in Brigham, L et al (eds) (2000) *Crossing Boundaries* Kidderminster, BILD

Over time, institutions became increasingly medicalised and clear hierarchies were established based on power structures which still hold sway today. Men and women were segregated and their lives strictly controlled to prevent procreation. In order to function, the institutions required a mix of abilities and people were allocated jobs according to their classified ability as high grade, medium grade or low grade. However, the distinction between the roles of the paid carers and 'patients' was not always evident since the latter undertook not only catering, cleaning, agricultural and industrial tasks but also care work, with more able people looking after less able (Mitchell, 2000; Atherton, 2003). Mitchell reports that 'a small number of people who had been classified as "mental defectives" went on to become probationer nurses' (p.126).

The traumatic accounts of older survivors from institutions give us some insight into what life was like in these places, even when regimes became looser. Jimmy still has very clear memories even though it is many years since he was 'released' (his word):

Part of Jimmy's story

When I was inside I went into a world of my own. I asked the charge nurse, 'When am I getting out of here?' The charge nurse said to me, 'The only way you'll get out of here is in a box.'

Because I'd live each day being without somebody, talking to somebody, because I've been inside too long I felt terrible.

You're in a world of your own. We had a tradition. One of the staff made it.
What would happen would be – Say S. was admitted into ward 3. Nobody would talk to him. Nobody would go near him. He would be asked to sit in a corner on his own for 48 hours. Nobody would be allowed to talk to him, or sit down beside him, for two days.

They were treated terribly because they weren't allowed to – well, there's one person I'll not forget. She was like a sergeant-major. Everybody had to sit in one room and weren't allowed to talk at all. She shouted at them all the time. And there's us sitting there as quiet as anything the whole day.

I wasn't allowed to go to school. The school teacher phoned up and said, 'Are there any other boys who could go to school? There's one desk empty'. And the charge nurse said nobody here can go. The teacher said, 'Bring him down'. The charge nurse said, 'No, we can't bring him down – he doesn't know anything. He can't do anything'. And when I went down there, the teacher gave me this book and I was straight into it. It was great. Being able to do things, school work and that.

We never spoke to each other (the children) – we never interacted with each other. The staff always kept us apart. I made one friend – Tommy P. We played together and talked together. Yes. We were great friends, me and Tommy.

Many people had no idea why they ended up in such places. Harry, who was 79 when he was finally released from the long-stay hospital where he'd been since he was six, told me, 'I think they took me there because I wasn't very good at crossing the road and they thought I might have an accident. I remember the van came and it was a long journey. They took me into the ward with all the other children but they weren't allowed to speak to me. You had to do what they told you. You knew better than to argue. I kept quiet because I didn't want any trouble. They were bad times. Very bad times. I don't like to think about them now.'

Barron (2000) describes his admission to an institution after being taken away from an abusive foster mother at the age of eleven: 'I was taken away by two burly men – I was told by these people ... that simply because I was being severely beaten up where a foster mother was paid to look after me, practically starving me to death, that's why I was put in this mental hospital' (p.11). He recalls an attendant with a 'big long dog chain' taking him to a ward where all the windows had bars and the doors were locked, where people sat around the ward, where the door was locked while he was given a bath. He also remembers ward 1, the punishment ward, where 'patients' were sent to scrub the concrete floor with cold water regardless of the weather and had their rations cut from two slices to half a slice of bread. He writes too of the sexual abuse he experienced.

Barron remained affected by his institutional experiences, saying, 'I've still got my memories and the pain. I sometimes find it hard being alone after so many years of being with others, never having to think for yourself, doing what you were told. I've got to watch that I don't slip back into institutional ways... to this day, in my little flat, I still turn my bed down, ready for inspection!' (Barron, 1996, p.122).

Mabel Cooper went to St Lawrence's in 1952 when she was seven. She recalls: 'There was bars on the windows when I first went to St Lawrence's, it was just like a prison. Of course it was called a nuthouse in them days, so it used to have bars on it. You couldn't open the windows. Well, you could, but not far enough to get out of them. You didn't have no toys, no toys whatsoever ... The ward was blocked off, there was doors. You weren't allowed to sit on your beds. The beds were that close to one another, so you couldn't have anything private' (Atkinson et al, 1997).

In *The Empty Hours*, Oswin (1971) provides a harrowing account of the lives of children in institutions in England. In *Revisiting the Empty Hours* (2000), she reminds us: 'It is very important that we remember these children who lived in the Special Care Wards. ... Today, when most long-stay hospitals have been shut and people are living in the community and are telling their stories, there are those who can describe their earlier lives and say: "I spent years living in an institution, I was very deprived." They can put their hands up and say, "Remember my story." But the children I worked with will never be able to put up their hands and tell their stories. When the final history of the old Mental Handicap hospitals is written not one of those people with multiple disabilities who grew up in Special Care Wards will be able to stand up and say what it was like to be deprived for so long, to be so excluded, so forgotten by society' (p.141).

Stainton (2000) accurately describes the period as 'arguably one of the darkest periods in the history of people considered to have some form of learning disability' (p.89) and 'the transition from a period of relatively humane paternalism to active suppression and control' (p.90). The 1912 Bill, which resulted in the 1913 Mental Deficiency Act, Stainton says, marked the dominance of the state over the lives of people with learning disabilities.

You might like to read . . .

'From community to institution – and back again' by David Barron, in Brigham, L. et al (eds) (2000) *Crossing Boundaries* Kidderminster, BILD

'Mabel Cooper's Life Story' in Atkinson et al (eds) (1997) *Forgotten Lives: Exploring the History of Learning Disability* Kidderminster, BILD

'Using Oral Histories' by Fido and Potts in Atkinson et al (eds) (1997) *Forgotten Lives: Exploring the History of Learning Disability* Kidderminster, BILD

The Empty Hours by Maureen Oswin (1971), London, Penguin Press

---

For a long time, the only records we had of life in institutions were those from official sources which, inevitably, put the official view. At that time there was a belief that when people were moved from long-stay hospitals to life in the community their institutional experiences were best forgotten because of the pain it caused them. However, people have said very clearly that they want to reclaim their past history and our understanding has been greatly enhanced by personal accounts of life in an institution. Fido and Potts (1997) report that they were more overtly horrified by the accounts of former residents they interviewed than were the people themselves, saying: 'Having suffered a lifetime of being downgraded and discriminated against, the contributors' immediate response was in fact to be encouraged at having their experiences recognised' (p.45).

In the foreword to *Forgotten Lives: Exploring the History of Learning Disability* (Atkinson et al, eds, 1997) Taylor writes: 'In all the work being done, in all the money being spent on the shift from institutional to community-based services for people with learning disabilities, there was no real sense of history. Charred scraps of paper, containing clues to the reality of the lives of thousands, were dancing over the bonfires of closing institutions. No records were being kept, no photographs of the

ACTIVITY 1: **Media watch**

Attitudes have changed substantially since then, but public perception of
people with learning disabilities is still influenced by perceptions in the past.
To explore one aspect of this, undertake a 'media watch'. Over the next few
weeks, pay particular attention to the ways in which people with learning
disabilities are represented in local and national newspapers, magazines,
radio and television – and in films, if relevant. Keep notes on any negative
descriptions or references you encounter – terminology, assumptions
and so on.

You might want to respond to some of the things you hear by writing to
the publication or programme. You may already have done this, of course,
on other occasions.

You might also like to include the staff and service users in this type of
activity (if you don't already do this) and in ways of combating these
negative images. It can be useful to get local radio stations and newspapers
involved in portraying positive images and carrying positive reports, as long
as these aren't patronising.

wards, no biographies of the people, not even a home video of the bonfire... In our
work in teaching paid staff in community settings, we noticed over and over again
that they had very little awareness of what life had been like for disabled people in
the earlier decades of this century, and only a limited understanding of the reasons
for change. The books concerned with these issues could be counted on one hand.
Collectively, we seemed determined to eliminate the past and leave no trace of
the present.'

Comment

Negative images of people with learning disabilities are perpetuated by the media
much more than we sometimes realise. Getting into the habit of 'media watching'
can be useful, but it has to be handled sensitively, especially if you are doing this in
partnership with people with learning disabilities or family members.

Some thoughts from Marion about perceptions of people with learning disabilities

There are people who don't understand what it is like to have the difficulties and they don't waste time with you, and just put it off – you're classed as a disabled person – they don't have the time to understand that you have difficulties with reading and writing and sometimes you're embarrassed. People don't really understand what causes these things, and they don't spend much time with you to help you to read. That's why the class is helping me – to help me with my reading and writing. If it wasn't for the classes I wouldn't be able to read or write. So I feel that if people understood more about people with learning difficulties it would help them more.

It makes you feel angry, like nobody wants to understand you, that you've just got a label across you, and it makes you feel downhearted – you know, come on, listen here – I've got learning difficulties – you don't understand these things – you don't understand why I've got learning difficulties. It comes from your family background, but you don't understand, I can't read and I can't write. But some people do understand now, because I'm going to the classes. But other people don't.

Before I couldn't, but now I can, and I can read some types of newspaper, and things like that. It makes me feel good, it makes me feel – I've done it myself, nobody's helped me, I've done this myself, and it's good for me to do, I say to myself. And that's why people have to understand that for people with learning difficulties it's hard to understand. And that's why the classes have been good to me. I've maybe not been going every week, because family problems have cropped up, but when I do go I feel I have to catch up on different things, which are written out for me, so I feel it's quite helpful.

From institutions to community care

As Felce et al (1998) put it, 'The roots of any reform lie in the prevailing circumstances that precede it' (p.7). Institutionalisation in England and Wales increased from about 17,100 to about 51,200 places between 1924 and 1944 and subsequently to around 65,000 places (DHSS 1971a, 1972; Ayer and Alaszewski, 1984 in Felce et al, 1998).

No one force was responsible for the social change which led to a rethink of service provision. 'The movement towards reform derived from a variety of factors which were felt in various ways in much of the developed world' (Felce et al, 1998, p.7). Among these factors were:

- the growth of human and civil rights movements which challenged oppression and social injustice and which led to new policies, including the European Convention on Human Rights

- the development of sociological theories relating to devalued groups, eg the work of Erving Goffman, in which he contended that people regarded as 'deviant' adopt the roles ascribed to them by society, thus perpetuating and reinforcing the stereotypical beliefs of others

- changes in legislation, including the 1959 Mental Health Act which advocated an end to the compulsory certification of people with learning disabilities, meaning that those detained with no legitimate reason could be discharged back into the community (and replaced the term 'mental deficiency' with 'mental subnormality')

- changes in perceptions of people labelled 'subnormal', eg the work of O'Connor and Tizard in the 1950s, showing that many people in the institutions previously thought incapable of employment could in fact learn work related skills; and the work of Clarke and Clarke (1959) who drew attention to the relationship between stimulating environments and performance ability

- the 1971 White Paper, *Better Services for the Mentally Handicapped*, calling for an end to custodial care, advocated a 50% reduction in institutionalised places by 1991 and retraining of staff (Atkinson et al, 1997; Felce et al, 1998; Atherton, 2003)

- hospital scandals, such as those at Ely and Harperbury, which uncovered abuse and exploitation

Terminology over this period reflects the changing ideology: institutions became hospitals, patients became residents and wards became villa. Schools inside the institutions gradually closed and children went out to special schools, returning to the hospital in the evening. But large numbers of people remained in the long-stay hospitals.

The principles of normalisation

Probably one of the most important influences of the time was that of *normalisation*, which still influences service provision today. Normalisation originated in Denmark as part of the 1959 Mental Retardation Act and advocated 'an existence for the mentally retarded as close to normal living conditions as possible' (Bank-Mikkleson, 1980, in Felce et al, 1998). The concept was developed further at that time in Sweden (Nirje, 1980) but was later criticised on the grounds that, although its aim was to promote equal rights, it did not advance integration. However, as Felce et al (1998, p.11) point out, it was a significant development, one which other countries had not yet arrived at, and it 'highlighted access to normal patterns of living for all, regardless of level of disability: a commitment which was not found in Britain until stated as one of the determining principles of the AWS' (All Wales Strategy, 1983).

In the USA Wolfensberger adopted a more sociological perspective to normalisation, redefining it as the 'utilisation of means which are as culturally normative as possible in order to establish and/or maintain personal behaviours and characteristics which are as culturally normative as possible' (Wolfensberger, 1972 in Atherton, 2003). Normalisation addresses such issues as rights, individuality, development, culture- and age-appropriateness, social integration and typical patterns of living and uses these as criteria against which services and their impact can be evaluated. The role of services is to establish socially valued roles for people who are devalued within society, to counteract labelling and devalued roles and to improve personal competence. By doing this, they can promote the acceptance of service users by the wider society (Knapp et al, 1992; Means and Smith, 1994; Felce et al, 1998; Atherton, 2003). It's notable that the emphasis is on services, not on people's lives.

In 1982, Wolfensberger and Tullman explained 'The principle of normalisation first appeared in North America in the late 1960s (Wolfensberger, 1980). Since then it has evolved into a systematic theory that can be used as a universal guiding principle in the design and conduct of human services, but which is especially powerful when applied to services to people who are devalued by the larger society'. They add: '...we use the following simple definition: Normalisation implies, as much as possible, the use of culturally valued means in order to enable, establish and/or maintain valued social roles for people' (p.138).

Wolfensberger later preferred the term 'social role valorisation' (SRV), one which he believes reflects our society more accurately, including the fact that some roles are more highly valued than others and other roles devalued. The contention is that people with learning disabilities are seen as negatively 'different', as a result are then segregated and denied access to ordinary living and socially valued roles, which in turn further devalues them. If they are to lead ordinary lives they must have access to socially valued roles. An important aspect of normalisation and SRV is the right of people with learning disabilities to experience the norms of everyday life (the routines of the day and of the week) and of the life cycle (events that mark childhood, adolescence and adulthood), and the right to relationships and to an acceptable standard of living.

As well as being highly influential, normalisation has been heavily criticised, not least because of its value base which accepts inequality within society and ignores the root causes of social injustice and exclusion. Its principles are also said to be based on the norms of middle class society. Also, it focuses on services rather than inclusion. Walmsley and Downer (1997) highlight gender blindness within normalisation which 'denied women with learning difficulties access to a knowledge of feminism, and tied them into conventional, often subordinate, roles' (p.39). It has also, they contend, done little to address racism, heterosexism or sexism and may even have fostered them. Also, the implication is that disabled people are not 'normal'. 'The emphasis in normalisation on the value of relationships with people who are not disabled tends to devalue disabled people' (p.30).

I agree wholeheartedly with these points. When normalisation was at its height in the UK, I had great difficulty with its philosophy, especially with the implication that disabled people, just as they were, were somehow of less value than others and had to change to become more valued. This seemed to be a contradiction of what the principle professed to be about. People moving out of long-stay hospitals were losing touch with lifetime friends – often the only people who made life bearable – and being encouraged to get to know and spend time with people who were considered more 'valued'. I have always had a great deal of difficulty with the jargon associated with normalisation as any philosophy which cannot be put into straightforward English and made accessible to those it seeks to support is flawed. One reason for this, of course, is that normalisation was not developed *with* people with learning disabilities but *for* them.

Despite all this, most people acknowledge that normalisation was, for its time, a significant development. It has been one of the most powerful influences on service development in recent times and continues to affect what we do.

In the UK, the principles of normalisation were developed by O'Brien and Tyne (1981) into the 'five service accomplishments': community presence, choice, competence, respect and community participation. These accomplishments provided a framework against which services could operate and help people with learning disabilities achieve an 'ordinary life' (Atherton, 2003). Research from the King's Fund and the publication *An Ordinary Life* (1980) were instrumental in moving things forward.

Reflection

Reflect on the service in which you work and the way in which it operates. To what extent can you see the influences of normalisation and ordinary life principles in the way in which the service functions? How do you feel about this?

Legislation and policy developments

There are several policy documents, White Papers and Acts of Parliament that influenced service development in the second half of the twentieth century. These include:

- the 1970 Education Act (England & Wales) under which children with learning disabilities became the responsibility of the Education Authority rather than Health. Junior training centres were redesignated schools and staff with qualifications from the Health Authority were recognised as qualified teachers on completion of a probationary period. Children with learning disabilities were assigned to either ESN (M) (Educationally Subnormal, Mild or Moderate) or ESN (S) (Educationally Subnormal, Severe) schools on the basis of assessment. Children with profound and multiple disabilities were placed into 'special care' units in ESN (S) schools

- the formation of the National Development Group in 1975 to advise on policy and practice

- the publication of the Warnock Report in 1978 which advocated the integration of some, but not all, children with 'special needs' in mainstream schools

- the Jay Report in 1979 which advocated provision in community based settings

- the 1981 Education Act (England and Wales) which said that children should be educated in mainstream schools wherever possible

- the All Wales Strategy for Mentally Handicapped People (1983) which promoted ordinary lifestyles for people with learning disabilities in Wales and was the first national strategy in the UK

- the 1988 Disabled Person's (Services consultations and Representations) Act

- the 1989 White Paper *Caring for People* which established the principles for:

- the NHS and Community Care Act in 1990, which provided the framework to enable people to stay in their own homes as long as possible and receive appropriate day, respite and domiciliary services. Social services in England and Wales and the Social Work Department in Scotland were given primary responsibility for carrying out community care assessments which should result in people receiving services tailored to their individual needs

- the 1995 Disability Discrimination Act, designed to protect the rights of all disabled people in relation to the purchase of goods and services, obstructions to the use of services, education, buying or renting property and employment

- the Human Rights Act (1998) which aims to protect the individual rights of everyone, disabled or non-disabled

Without a doubt the most significant recent developments in policy terms have been the White Paper *Valuing People* (DH, 2001), the review of services in Scotland documented in *The same as you?* (Scottish Executive 2000) and *Fulfilling the Promise* in Wales.

Individual planning

One of the most important things to emerge from this period was the acknowledgement of people with learning disabilities as individuals. Grant (1997, p.127) writes: 'Individual planning can be seen historically as an attempt to overcome the inherited problems of fragmented services, service-led provision and ill-defined systems of accountability' whose basic idea is to 'assist people who deliver services to focus on the unique needs of the individual receiving those services and to ensure that he or she has a major say in planning his or her life and determining the help he or she requires' (Blunden, Evans and Humphries, 1987)'. Individual Programme Planning (IPP) or Individual Planning (IP) was instituted as the most appropriative way of remedying these shortcomings, influenced by developments in the USA, particularly Individual Educational Plans (IEP). Individual planning was based on a particular set of principles, namely that:

- People with learning disabilities should be recognised first and foremost as individuals.

- People with learning disabilities (and, where relevant, their families) should be actively involved in the identification of their own needs and in any decisions about their own lives.

- The process should enable people to receive services tailored to their individual needs rather than expecting them to fit into existing services, ie service provision would be needs led rather than service led.

- Service provision should also enable multidisciplinary co-ordination.

Individual planning spawned a number of variants, among them the Open University *Shared Action Planning*, developed as part of the course *Mental Handicap: Patterns for Living* in 1986. Shared Action Planning re-emphasised the active involvement of the person with a learning disability and provided a mechanism for ensuring that he or she was a partner in the process.

Individual planning was one of the key features of the All Wales Strategy (AWS). The AWS had three guiding principles: the rights of everyone 'to normal patterns of life within the community, to be treated as individuals and to receive additional help from the communities in which they lived and from professional services in order to develop their maximum potential as individuals' (Felce et al, 1998, p.15). Reviewing the progress of the strategy, Felce et al identify several difficulties encountered in the implementation of individual planning, which include:

- the demands of the process in terms of time and resource commitments

- problems of consistency and sustainability, especially in relation to the ongoing process of reviewing and redefining direction

- promoting the meaningful inclusion of service users in decision making

Nevertheless, they go on to say: 'Knowledge about the best ways to involve people in making plans and making decisions about their lives was not widespread in 1983, but it is probably true to say that the AWS helped to set an agenda where these issues were taken much more seriously than before. There are now examples of people with learning disabilities being involved in the design and management of services, recruitment and training of staff, quality assurance and service evaluation, even if they remain uncommon in practice' (p.167).

As someone who was involved in various ways in the AWS, I recall it as a time of energy and considerable development for people with learning disabilities, despite its flaws. People were doing things they'd never done before. They were visible and participating. Many Day Centres were questioning their traditional roles and were becoming merely points of contact for people who were out doing other things. More people got jobs. Services without buildings were established. I know this didn't happen for everyone, but it did for a lot. J, for example, whose elderly mother died suddenly and left him on his own, was able to remain in his own home and was well supported through his grief and adaptation to his new circumstances; M, who moved into his own flat and had his own front door key for the first time in his life – what a change from hospital life; T, who moved out of the institution to live in a family placement; G, who had multiple disabilities and no speech but who, in his 'small-scale community-based day service' planned his own weekly programme with support from staff who were as eager to learn about new ways as he was. I also recall the first self-advocacy conference in Wales when groups came together and support workers were only allowed to attend if they were truly there in a support role.

Concluding comment

As remarked earlier, history is a good teacher. The history of people with learning disabilities has taught us that people with learning disabilities *can* speak for themselves – whether they do this in words or in some other way; that they have clear ideas and opinions about what they want and like – and for those who can't tell us themselves, there are family carers and other advocates who can; that what is important to them is what is important to everyone else – relationships and a good standard of living, for example; that we are alike, sharing a common humanity. History also teaches us about the oppression people with learning disabilities have suffered in the past – something we must always guard against happening again. History can also help us shape the vision for the future, something we can work towards together.

From *Valuing People*

'Too many people with learning disabilities and their families still lead lives apart, with limited opportunities and poor life chances. To maintain the momentum of change we now need to open up mainstream services, not create further specialist services. People with learning disabilities should have the same opportunities as other people to lead full and active lives and should receive the support needed to make this possible' (p.17).

Chapter 2

The concept of learning disability

Introduction

The historical changes discussed in the previous chapter also mark changes in understanding. You only have to look at the way terminology has changed to get an idea of how our thinking has developed – language is a remarkable barometer of change. This second chapter is concerned particularly with changes in our understanding of learning disability. It's about the concept of learning disability – what it means and how our understanding of the term affects the kinds of support we provide.

The aim of this chapter is to discuss:

● current definitions of learning disability and the debates surrounding them

● learning disability as a spectrum

● the effects learning disability might have on physical, cognitive, social and emotional development

Definitions of learning disability

It's an interesting fact, although not surprising, that learning disability has traditionally been defined not by the people who experience it but by 'outsiders' – psychiatrists, psychologists, educationalists, theorists and researchers, for example. It's only relatively recently that we have woken up to the fact that perhaps there is something central missing from the equation – the perspectives of people with learning disabilities themselves and those closest to them. A survey in the early 1970s asked service users in what was then called an Adult Training Centre about their aspirations for the future and the ways in which they felt the centre could help them achieve these. This was ground-breaking stuff by a forward looking centre manager, but was regarded at the time as somewhat gimmicky and not to be taken seriously.

Definitions of, and responses to, learning disability throughout history have, as Gates and Wilberforce (2003) remark, 'reflected the dominant theoretical perspective that has been used at any one time in order to understand it' (p.9). The previous chapter illustrates this and it will continue to be true in the future.

Definitions can be useful, but they have limitations, especially where they relate to people, as Vlachou (1997) explains: 'definition is complex but significant, because definitions serve different, although interdependent, functions: they allow for communication, thought, social interaction and control ... That is, on the one hand they order individuals' personal and social experiences by offering an ideological framework within which people make sense of cultural, social and political phenomena. On the other hand they are devices for the transmission of these ideological frameworks, including perceptions and conceptualisations, between individuals. Thus, definitions become the means of making sense of the world around us, setting our histories and ideologies in context and providing a basis for generating action ... Because of their social function and the involvement of ideology, definitions include an inherent ambiguity and a conflicting multiplicity' (pp.10–11).

Gates and Wilberforce (2003) agree: 'Defining learning disability is much easier to talk about than it is to achieve. Understanding any concept, idea or phenomenon requires access to a prescribed language that expresses some common understanding amongst people as to what is being discussed. This is necessary for the development of knowledge, and the study of learning disability is no exception' (p.4). The salient issue is whose 'prescribed language' and whose 'common understanding' are we talking about?

Souza (1997) has no doubts about how she has been affected by being defined in a certain way: 'There were so many times that I might have entered the long road to a life defined by some people as being worth less than other members of society. I could all too easily have been created by others as a label and not a person. In fact, there have been some ways in which this was always, and still is, on the cards. If it had not been for the persons close to me fighting for my individuality and my rights to a normal life when I was young, I would certainly have fallen into this trap. If I had not myself recognised the issues as I grew up I might have been taken along on their tide of prejudice...

It takes a lot of courage and strength to fight against people who have the power to define what you are. People who think they can define you also assume they can tell you what your rights are and, because of who they think you are, specify what you should do with your life. They don't specify this by *telling* you what to do with your life only. It's worse than that. They put you in situations where there are only a limited range of things you can do with your life... When I was born my mother was told by the doctors that I had Down's syndrome and would be mentally and physically handicapped for the rest of my life. It was a very negative way to describe me and what my mum could expect from me. If it had not been for a nurse who told my mother that she could expect a lot of joy from me I think my mother would have been totally devastated' (p.4).

Souza, like everyone in her position, has had to fight for her right to be seen as a person first, included in the mainstream of society. Borland and Ramcharan (1997) describe her as a 'border crosser', crossing the boundary from a 'disabled identity' or 'excluded identity' to an 'identity as a person' or an 'included identity' within society. They say: 'apart from recognition that this (Down's syndrome) is a label attached to her by the medical profession, she otherwise argues that she is the same as anyone else, with the same sorts of needs and wishes as other members of society' (p.91).

You might like to read . . .

'Everything you Ever Wanted to Know About Down's Syndrome, but Never Bothered to Ask' by Anya Souza, (1997) in Ramcharan, P et al (eds) *Empowerment in Everyday Life*, London: Jessica Kingsley

---

The self-advocacy movement in the UK prefers the term 'learning difficulty' to 'learning disability', largely because people feel that the identification of a 'difficulty' with learning signifies that it is something that can be overcome, with the right kind of support and resource provision. This is true. However, 'learning disability', is the term in use officially in the UK. It also aligns more neatly with the social model of disability, ie understanding disability as a social phenomenon, arising from the structures and systems of society which are designed to safeguard and promote the status of its more privileged members and militate against those less powerful. The self-advocacy movement, on the other hand, is derived at least partly from normalisation, with its influence on labelling theory, valued and devalued roles within society. Among the people with learning disabilities I know there are differences of opinion about which 'label' is preferable – 'difficulties' or 'disabilities'. All of them prefer just to be known as themselves.

The term 'learning disability' is far from being a universal one. In fact it leads to confusion internationally. In the USA the term is used to describe specific learning disabilities such as dyslexia. Some countries and international bodies use 'intellectual disability' instead. In the USA the label 'mental retardation' is still widely used, although there are moves to change this to 'intellectual disability'. For example, the President's Committee on Mental Retardation, an advisory body providing advice to the US President and the Secretary of Health and Human Services, has been renamed as the President's Committee for People with Intellectual Disabilities. This was an attempt to 'eliminate the two words that create difficulties for people with "mental retardation". The word "mental" has often caused confusion with the term "mental illness" and the word "retardation" has often led to the use of offensive name-calling terms, eg "retard", "retarded", and "retardate". The Committee seeks to eliminate negative attitudes and promote a more positive image for people with intellectual disabilities among the general public and employers' (www.ach.hhs.gov).

How do you feel about trying to define 'learning disability'? Reflect on this for the next activity.

ACTIVITY 2: **What's in a definition?**

What are the negative aspects of having definitions of learning disabilities?

What are the positive aspects of having definitions of learning disabilities?

What ways of ensuring that definitions of learning disability are used constructively instead of destructively can you suggest?

Comment

For negative aspects of definitions, did you include any of the following?

- They can stigmatise people.

- They have a negative effect on other people's perceptions of the person defined.

- They quickly become common currency and can prevent people questioning what lies behind them.

- They can lead to stereotyping and discrimination.

- They categorise people, imply homogeneity and overlook individuality.

- They can perpetuate oppression, inequality and acceptance of the status quo.

- People are defined in terms of only one aspect of themselves and their 'personhood' is denied or overlooked.

For positive aspects of definitions, was anything on your list similar to the items below?

- They can help us to explore ideas and reach better understanding if used constructively.

- They can provide a common means of transmitting information and advancing knowledge.

- They can help the people concerned achieve a common voice and collective identity to challenge inequality and oppression.

- They can facilitate access to support and resources.

- They can be useful for families.

- They can lead to better legislation, policies and strategic planning, as well as targeted budgets.

Perhaps you decided that definitions in relation to learning disability are never positive.

How tricky did you find the third question? Here are some of the things you could have listed:

- Be aware when I have to resort to a definition, for whatever purpose, of how this affects the person I'm talking to.

- Avoid using definitions unless there isn't any other option.

- Be aware of the uniqueness and individuality of the person I'm referring to.

- Use people's names where possible and describe who they are, rather than focus on their learning disability, which is only one aspect and not the most important.

- Be aware of how the definition affects the way I think about people, eg influencing my expectations.

- Be aware of the effect of using the term 'learning disability' when I'm writing anything, eg reports and associated communications, or discussing matters relating to a particular person.

- Be aware of the misunderstandings that exist in relation to 'learning disability' in the public at large.

Do definitions help towards a concept of 'learning disability'?

One of the greatest drawbacks of trying to define 'learning disability' is the depersonalisation involved. After all, learning disability is only one aspect of the people we're concerned with. I often wonder how I'd feel if the only reason other people ever mentioned me was to discuss my intellectual ability – it's a bit horrifying! Learning disability can only really be understood within the context of the experiences of the people who know most about it – people with learning disabilities themselves and those closest to them.

There's been a considerable focus on 'intelligence', but does this help? Gates and Wilberforce (2003) write: 'Some would argue that intelligence is an obvious criterion on which to judge whether someone has a learning disability. An immediate problem with this is being able to decide just what intelligence is. ... it is assumed that intelligence is something to do with the ability to solve problems and that this ability, or the absence of it, can be measured. One way of measuring intelligence is by using intelligence tests. These tests have been used since the turn of the century; they serve the purpose of enabling one to measure the intellectual ability of one individual to complete a range of standardised tests against a large representative sample of the general population of a similar chronological age ...

Intelligence tests were used extensively during the 1960s and 1970s; however, recognition by psychologists and others of the many limitations of their use has made them less popular today. These limitations include cultural bias, poor predictive ability, and an incomprehensive relevance for the identification of learning disability. Despite the range of criticisms constructed against the use of intelligence tests, if they are used appropriately and by properly trained technicians then they do provide a relatively objective measure of the intellectual ability of an individual. In addition, if such a measure is used in conjunction with other criteria, such as social competence, this may be helpful in identifying whether or not an individual has learning disabilities' (pp.4–5).

Intellectual ability is undoubtedly one dimension of the concept of learning disability, but it isn't the only one, nor is it an easy one to define, as Gates and Wilberforce (above) point out. Recently, a friend who has an adult son with a profound learning disability said to me, 'I know it's a funny thing to say, but he's really clever in all sorts of ways.' I knew exactly what she meant, because he is. He's fascinated by the washing machine and can operate it independently. He's also great with the juke box his parents bought him for his eighteenth birthday – and the video and CD players. He's a bit of a 'gadget man' and has figured them all out by watching and learning. He shows a remarkable aptitude for solving problems when they're about things he's interested in (like the rest of us), especially technology. So what does that say about him in terms of intelligence – ability to adapt, figure things out, make sense of the world and so on? And how about his label of profound learning disability?

Like the rest of us, he's someone with his own unique and complex identity, his social networks, preferences and dislikes, dreams and aspirations. He's a brother, a son, an uncle, a friend, a neighbour, a user of services, both mainstream (the bus, the local doctor, the local shops), and specialist (for people with learning disabilities). He's male, adult and white. At times he becomes defined in particular ways – a holiday maker, a hospital inpatient. Learning disability is only one dimension of his identity and not necessarily the most important.

Gates and Wilberforce (2003) talk about the 'very wide nature and different manifestations of learning disabilities', reminding us: 'people with learning disabilities, regardless of the impact of those learning disabilities, share a common humanity with the rest of the population. Most people desire love and a sense of connection with others; they wish to be safe, to learn, to lead a meaningful life, to be free from ridicule and harm, to be healthy and free from poverty; and in this respect people with learning disabilities are no different (p.17). This is a good starting point for the rest of this discussion.

Reflection

How do you feel about having definitions of learning disability? Can you see conflicts with the philosophy of your service and your own philosophy? Are there times when definitions can be useful in your own work?

Learning disability as a spectrum

Learning disability is often referred to as a spectrum, ie there is no single cause or manifestation and there is a wide range. Learning disability can occur in isolation or exist alongside other impairments, such as physical or sensory. People described as having 'profound and multiple learning disabilities' have additional physical, hearing and visual impairments as well as cognitive impairment and usually have complex needs. The latter might include health needs such as epilepsy. In the UK learning disabilities are often categorised as mild, moderate, severe or profound. Many people question both the validity and the usefulness of such distinction. There's the ethical dilemma of categorising people, touched upon in the previous chapter. Also, one person may have marked difficulties with certain skills, but be very capable in others. Supporters of categorisation contend that it's the learning disability that is being categorised and not the person, but this is difficult to defend since it's impossible to separate people from their characteristics. There is an argument that distinguishing between different degrees of learning disability helps us identify needs more clearly and provide better support. To an extent I can see the reasoning behind this, but surely this is more effectively done by getting to know the person better and listening to his or her aspirations? In fact, the categorisation of learning disability is an official device and the concept of 'need' a professional construct. Both are fast becoming discredited and replaced by more person centred approaches based on rights and entitlement.

More *person centred* approaches do not deny an individual's learning disability, nor the fact that the individual requires support, but they do approach it from an entirely different philosophical stance – one that starts with the individual rather than an objective definition which relates to only one aspect of the human being behind the label. The majority of people with learning disabilities *do* need support to achieve what they want in life. Sometimes this support is required because of the difficulties people have in learning the things the rest of us take for granted; sometimes it's required because of the way in which they are oppressed within society (discussed in more detail in chapter 5 and referred to at other places in this book). Often it's a combination of the two. Philosophically, there's no difference in this respect between people with learning disabilities and everyone else.

I'm hopeless at crosswords (often thought to be a sign of intellectual ability) and not too keen on jigsaws. My technological skills are far less developed than many primary school children. I need to call on the 'experts' when I want my car serviced or my washing machine repaired. Like everyone else, there are areas in my life where I'm independent and others where I'm *interdependent*. So how would you classify my intellectual capacity?

Diversity within the concept of 'learning disability'

The diversity within the concept of the term 'learning disability' is reflected in the way in which different individuals experience learning disability, but also in the way in which the term is used. Use the following activity to explore the meaning usually ascribed to the term 'learning disability'.

ACTIVITY 3: **The meaning of 'learning disability'**

People use different criteria for determining whether or not someone has a learning disability. Read through these explanations of 'learning disability' and then undertake the task that follows.

1. In *Valuing People* (DoH, 2001, p.14) learning disability is explained thus: '*Learning disability includes the presence of:*

● *a significantly reduced ability to understand new or complex information, to learn new skills (impaired intelligence) with;*

● *a reduced ability to cope independently (impaired social functioning);*

● *which started before adulthood, with a lasting effect on development.*'

2. In *The same as you?* the report on the review of services for people with learning disabilities in Scotland (Scottish Executive, 2000, p.3), this is the explanation given:

'*People with learning disabilities have a significant, lifelong condition that started before adulthood, that affected their development and which means they need help to:*

● *understand information*

● *learn skills; and*

● *cope independently*'

3. The World Health Organisation (WHO) defines learning disabilities as:

● '*a state of arrested or incomplete development of mind*'

Somebody with a learning disability is said also to have:

● '*significant impairment of intellectual functioning*'

● '*significant impairment of adaptive/social functioning*'

Task
Identify any similarities in two or all three of these explanations.

Which of the explanations fits most neatly with your own understanding of 'learning disability' and why?

Comment

Did you identify these common features?

- Learning disability is a lifelong condition (first two explanations).

- The difficulty should be 'significant' (all three).

- 'Intelligence' is mentioned in two.

- All three mention ability to cope socially.

- The first two mention ability to understand information and that learning disability starts before adulthood.

There are more similarities in the first two explanations than there are with the third. This isn't really surprising, since the WHO is an international body which is trying to incorporate the perspectives of different countries. Given that it's impossible to agree on terminology, it's unlikely to be easy to find an explanation all countries can agree on. I certainly feel much less comfortable with the WHO explanation than I do with the other two, especially its negative emphasis on a '*state of arrested or incomplete development of mind*'.

The first two explanations are the ones currently in use in the UK.

The concept of learning disability encompasses considerable diversity, much of which has nothing to do with intellect. Walmsley and Downer (1997) remind us that: 'the term (learning disabilities) includes people with many different social characteristics and abilities, and sometimes various medical conditions. Research studies have shown that it is more common for people of lower social classes (Rutter and Madge, 1976) and for black people (Bryan, Dadzie and Scafe, 1985) to be given the label of special educational needs or learning difficulties. However, specific syndromes such as Down syndrome affect people from all social classes... There was until recently a failure by researchers and practitioners to recognise that people with this label also have identities as men and women, black or white people, Jewish or Moslem, and hetero- or homosexual, indeed as working, middle or upper class.... it is not safe to assume that people who have the same label will necessarily have identical interests or be able to represent others adequately' (p.38).

People with learning disabilities are often referred to in literature as if they were a homogeneous group (Gates and Wilberforce, 2003). This is misleading and simplistic, ignores individuality and uniqueness, constrains thinking and denies individual people the opportunities they are entitled to. In a project involving young people with learning disabilities from a south Asian background, Maudslay et al (2003) found that participants stressed the importance of their religion and culture more than their learning disability. They were fully aware of the differences between their own ethnic group and others from south Asia, eg Pakistani and Bangladeshi. Like the rest of us, people with learning disabilities are diverse in terms of personality, age, ability, experience, culture and other characteristics.

The impact of learning disability on individuals

The diversity discussed earlier is also relevant when it comes to the impact of a learning disability on the person concerned. As Souza says, the effects depend on a number of things in addition to the learning disability itself, most notably other people's perceptions and expectations and how these affect opportunities for learning. Thus, the effect of a learning disability will depend on:

- the nature of the learning disability and the extent of the underlying impairment which causes or contributes to the learning disability

- family support

- the opportunities made available to the person concerned

- the support networks and resources available to that person

---

ACTIVITY 4: **The impact of learning disability**

Describe briefly someone you know who has a learning disability, selecting only what you consider to be relevant information.

In what ways has learning disability affected this person's life negatively?

Have these effects been the result of the learning disability itself, or have other factors caused them or contributed?

If there are other factors involved what are they and what is their effect?

In what ways has learning disability affected this person's life positively?

Comment

You might have mentioned that the person you wrote about has difficulty doing certain things because of particular difficulties with learning. But you probably also identified negative effects which, although connected with the learning disability, are more about other people's attitudes and responses. We know enough now to have realised that people with learning disabilities, whatever the extent of their disability, can lead productive and fulfilling lives if they have the right opportunities and supports in place. For some, especially those with profound and multiple learning disability, life might be very different from the one we live, or would like to live, but that's nothing unusual. Plenty of people live lives that are different, but no less valid!

Like everyone else, people with learning disabilities have strengths as well as weaknesses, some of which are undoubtedly derived from their learning disabilities. For example, people who have communication difficulties associated with learning disability often have to persevere to make themselves understood. This can mean they become extremely skilled in communicating in ways other than through words, which in turn, may help them develop skills the rest of us lack – insights into other people's more subtle signs in communication, for example. Whether this is a direct consequence of having a learning disability, or a combination of personality and the learning disability is a moot point.

The physical, cognitive, social and emotional effects of learning disability

I have to admit to considerable unease when it comes to discussing the effects of learning disability on people's learning and development. Part of me is aware that a better understanding of learning disability can help us improve support, but another part of me shies away from a focus on learning as a problem. I'm sure you share this dilemma with me, and I expect it's something we have to live with, for the present anyway. I'm also certain that, like me, you've more often been surprised by people's *abilities* rather than their difficulties.

To an extent, our understanding of the effects of learning disability on people's lives *does* have significance for the nature of the support we provide for them. Marion, for example, who's in her forties, has always regretted the fact that she never learned to read. She's now attending an adult literacy class where the tutor needs to identify her difficulties, as well as her strengths, in order to help her progress. The important issues, therefore, are how and where we provide the support, as well as who defines the needs and the aspirations. In many ways, it's easier to discuss this in relation to children, rather than adults, since children are expected to have their learning needs assessed and responded to. The context is also relevant – identifying the causes of a particular difficulty in an adult education setting has a clearly defined purpose.

We know that learning disability is associated with cognitive impairment and affects cognitive development, but the extent depends on a variety of factors. Thus it can affect the development of children because they might:

- have difficulty in processing information due to problems in attention, selecting information, making sense of what they see or hear and associating it with things they already know; these difficulties may cause information processing to take longer or to be incomplete; in general, the more abstract the information or more complex the concept, the more difficult it will be (not surprisingly – think of the difference between playing chess or playing dominoes, or of finding the answer to $1 + 2 = ?$ as opposed to $3(x + 5m) – 2m(y+4x) = ?$)

- have difficulties with language acquisition and development, eg be slower to talk, take longer to absorb and process verbal information

- have difficulties with articulation which may, or may not, be associated with muscular control or other aspects of physical development

- have difficulties with memory, eg retaining or retrieving information; recalling events or details; recognising things from previous experience

- find it difficult making associations between events and ideas, eg comparisons and similarities

- have the ability to transfer the skills used in one situation to other situations requiring the same or similar skills

- have the ability to adapt to different situations or tasks demanding adaptation of skills (as above) or behaviours (this can affect social situations, eg knowing the 'social rules' of different situations – church or temple as opposed to the playground; other people's homes as opposed to your own home; rules for touching and showing affection)

I've identified only some of the difficulties which might occur, the ones I think might have most significance for support work. Not everyone will experience all of these difficulties, of course, and the extent of the difficulty will be affected by the severity of the person's cognitive impairment. Thus people with additional physical, visual and hearing disabilities will face challenges in learning that might be more a result of their inability to interact with their environment rather than cognitive capacity.

The extent to which a learning disability affects someone in adult life depends both on the severity of the impairment, but also on the support provided and the learning opportunities made available throughout life. Complex disabilities which limit opportunity to interact with the environment can reduce people's learning opportunities, but it is the responsibility of service providers not just to accept this but to find ways of providing active support. The more skilled we become in providing the right kind of support, the less severe the effect of the impairment. Lancioni et al (2002) taught two children with profound and multiple learning disabilities to use multiple microswitches to control stimulation in their environment, eg animal noises, vibratory stimulation on body or chair, children talking, rhymes, musical instruments, light fibre compositions, etc and found that the children increased their activity level and 'constructive engagement with their surroundings' (p. 350).

Also, learning takes on a different shape as we reach adulthood. Like me, I'm sure you spent many tears learning things at school which play no part in your adult life. The same is true of people with learning disabilities.

The implications for support workers of knowing about possible cognitive difficulties are that it makes them more likely to:

- allow enough time for people to process information

- present information in more appropriate formats, such as pictures

- make sure people have enough time to learn new skills and to practise them

- break things down into manageable 'chunks' to help people absorb information

- be alert to feedback, verbal or otherwise and help people develop ways of signalling lack of understanding

- take the lead from the person concerned and allowing him or her to dictate the pace

These are easier things to do in educational settings with children, but trickier in ordinary, everyday situations – sometimes it's about slowing down the pace of life, but mostly it's about getting to know people and building a relationship of mutual trust, whatever the level of difficulty experienced by the person and the worker.

We also know that people with learning disabilities are more likely than others to have additional impairment, such as visual or hearing difficulties. In a review of literature concerned with learning disability and visual impairment across several countries, Warburg (2001) found that the prevalence of visual impairment in adults with learning disability was 'very high', that there was insufficient training of practitioners, as well as negative attitudes and value judgements about the worth of people with learning disabilities: 'The insufficient treatment of ophthalmic and optometric conditions in people with ID (intellectual disability) is similar in all countries from where information is available. Normalisation, decentralisation of care and community living depend a great deal on good vision, particularly when understanding what happens in the neighbourhood is difficult. It is astonishing and certainly unethical that disorders which are common, well described, easy to diagnose and for which inexpensive treatment is available have been left untreated in our affluent societies' (p.436).

Impairments which cause learning disability can also affect physical development. Children might be slower to reach childhood 'milestones' such as sitting unaided, crawling, walking, becoming continent and so on (although the question of 'milestones' in childhood is in itself something that's under debate). Muscle tone can be affected, such as in Down syndrome.

Language and cognitive capacity are closely linked. An important campaign by people with learning disabilities is the one against jargon – something all professionals are fond of! One woman I know regularly pulls us up short at meetings by reminding us, 'No jargon words!' while another makes a point of repeating the word and asking, very deliberately, 'What does that mean?' Timely reminders, since jargon reinforces divisions – although it can provide useful shortcuts at times.

Sometimes we assume that the difficulty experienced is as a result of cognitive ability when it is in fact about language, communication and our own assumptions. Hogg et al (2001) found considerable difference in opinion between service providers asked to decide whether adults with profound and multiple learning disabilities were expressing negative or positive emotions, even though the people were well known to them. Bradshaw (2001) compared staff reports of their communication with adults with learning disabilities with video observations of the communication. She found that staff were inclined to underestimate their use of verbal communication and overestimate their use of non-verbal communication. She also identified a mismatch between the reported level of understanding of the service user and the level of complexity of the language used. She concluded that staff 'appeared unable to adapt their communication to the skills of the service user and an average of 45% of communicative acts were outside the reported understanding of the individual' (p.233). While acknowledging the limitations of her study, she suggests that overestimation of people's understanding, as well as disregard for context and the low use of alternative and augmentative communication, contribute to the problems. Kevan (2003) also highlights the mismatch between the receptive language ability of some people with learning disabilities and the expressive communication of support staff. McConkey et al (1999) found that staff overestimate service users' comprehension, underestimate hearing problems and make too much use of verbal and instructional language even with people with the most profound intellectual impairment.

Situations we don't understand can be frightening, but as adults we learn strategies for overcoming these. People with learning disabilities don't always have access to such strategies. And how do you 'just walk away' if you have cerebral palsy and can't move without help? How do you explain your fears and frustrations if you don't have the words to describe them? Kevan (2003) reminds us that challenging behaviour is very often the result of a communicative environment that is confusing, rouses anxiety and is overwhelming or threatening, and that the message may be 'I want to escape'.

Some conditions, such as autism, mean that children find relationships difficult. Also, because children with a learning disability may develop more slowly than their peers; they may not have the skills to join in games, so relationships can suffer. This is less about the child's learning disability than the responses of other children and the social environment, but is often construed as being the result of the learning disability – which is why inclusive education, where children grow together, is so important.

This has relevance for emotional development. Arthur (2003) writes: 'The emotional lives and emotional difficulties of people with learning disabilities have been largely neglected and submerged by the behavioural technologies of the 1970s and 1980s. Incarcerated in large subnormality hospitals until the 1980s, people with learning disabilities in the UK were out of sight and out of mind' (p.26). Like everyone else, people with learning disabilities have complex emotional lives. We know that many are lonely, with few friends. Even people who have lived at home with their families all their lives have difficulty making and maintaining friendships and more intimate relationships, not because of their inability to do so, but because of lack of opportunity. Segregated services exacerbate this.

Emotional difficulties arise for people with learning disabilities for the same reasons as for everyone else – separation, loss, confusion, fear, anxiety and the whole gamut of life experiences. The situation is compounded by:

- segregated special schools which take people out of their own neighbourhoods and deny them the chance to attend the local school with their brothers and sisters

- negative attitudes towards people with learning disabilities within society

- our tendency to rate friendships with non-disabled people more highly than those with disabled people

- our inability to support people through grief and loss

- people's own difficulties in communicating their emotions and our lack of ability to understand emotions expressed in ways we are unaccustomed to

- underestimating people's responses to situations which cause emotional pain

- mistaking protection for support

From *Valuing People*

Helping people sustain friendships is consistently shown as being one of the greatest challenges faced by learning disability services. Good services will help people with learning disabilities to form relationships, including ones of a physical and sexual nature (p.81).

Concluding comment

We know that people with learning disabilities need support for certain things – just as we all do. If we get hung up on their difficulties we are doing them and ourselves a grave disservice. However, if understanding the difficulties they have in learning certain things helps us to provide the support they need to do the things they want, this can be productive and can help us help them to get a better life. Emphasis on interdependence and services which support, rather than segregate is what we need.

Chapter 3

The current context of support services

Introduction

This chapter considers the current context of services for people with learning disabilities with particular reference to empowerment, advocacy and social inclusion. The issues are:

- How do empowerment, advocacy and social inclusion relate to service development?

- What are the implications for service provision and development?

- How do current legislation and policy relate to service development?

The concept of empowerment

One of the problems of more complex concepts like empowerment is that they are subject to myriad interpretations. Ramcharan and Borland (1997) identify a number of meanings of the term from a range of authorities:

- consumer rights within a free market (Saunders, 1993)

- a means of preventing oppression (Ward and Mullender, 1991)

- people working to gain control of their own lives (Adams, 1990)

- people using self-help strategies (Jack, 1995)

- full citizenship rights through autonomy and self-determination and the achievement of minimum standards of well-being (Rioux, 1994)

- the democratisation of decision-making and participation (North, 1993) (cited in Ramcharan and Borland, 1997)

They go on to say: 'It may be argued that the complexion of the term "empowerment" is largely the complexion of its user... it has entered the language of professionals, tripping lightly off the tongue as a rationalisation for virtually any of their work for, or with, people with disabilities.'

McNally (2003) says: 'There is a danger that empowerment, a term which has passed into common usage and is applied in many contexts, could be disregarded as a buzz-word or taken to denote the token involvement of service users' (p.504).

This is an important point. The danger is that we become so accustomed to the word "empowerment" that, instead of recognising and harnessing it as a powerful force for change, it loses its dynamism. If we understand empowerment only at the level of social justice – the responsibilities of the state towards its citizens – we can stop at the level of rhetoric and easily ignore our own responsibilities and our own disempowering beliefs and practices. If, on the other hand, we are satisfied with only incremental change we can lose sight of the ultimate vision of a just and equitable society – and the process of getting there.

The representation of empowerment as a multidimensional concept is an important one in support services for people with learning disabilities. Empowerment is at one and the same time a philosophy, a continuous process, a vision and a goal. As a process it will never be complete. The vision will develop and the goal will be continually restated as our understanding develops and we make progress.

Empowerment relates primarily to the unequal distribution of power within society and the social model of disability (discussed in chapter 5). But we need also to be aware of the ways in which such power structures can be recreated through service structures and through our own practices, wittingly or unwittingly. McNally (2003) writes: 'It's been said that it's easier to explain how people become disempowered than how they become empowered and that "Empowerment is easier to define in its absence" (Rappaport, 1984): powerlessness, real or imagined; learned helplessness; alienation; loss of a sense of control over one's life.'

Souza (with Ramcharan, 1997) discusses disempowerment in terms of four separations. The first separation begins at birth by disabled people being marked out as negatively different: 'All of a sudden the doctor has separated me out, put a label on me, made everything to do with me a negative image' (p.4).

This rings many bells with me. Among them are:

- the mother of a two-month-old baby with Down syndrome who said to the home support worker, 'You're the first person who's said anything positive about my baby'

- the doctor who had to be reminded by a mother when he said, 'Peter (her second son) is a beautiful child', that, 'Yes, and so is Matthew (her first son who is disabled)'

- the parents who received many birth congratulations cards for their first child but only one, from grandparents, for their second baby who had Down syndrome

The second separation, according to Souza, comes at the time of formal education – schools which separate out 'people like me', moving them away from ordinary life.

The third separation comes at the time of transition to adult life. The fourth is separation from the workplace. There are clear parallels here with the idea of people with learning disabilities being confined to a separate life path, one which increasingly removes them from ordinary life. This highlights the link between disempowerment and social exclusion.

Borland and Ramcharan (1997) explore the notions of 'excluded' and 'included' identities in relation to empowerment. Exclusion from the experiences and structures of everyday life socialises people into an excluded self-concept and identity (as it would with any of us). Stigmatisation and discrimination lead to and perpetuate exclusion. Empowerment requires processes and experiences which make it possible for people with learning disabilities to develop an *included* identity. These authors suggest that, 'empowerment should be viewed as a system of interdependencies between people, institutions and structures' (p.95). This will only be achieved through systems and structures which provide opportunities for people with learning disabilities to be part of, and fully included in, ordinary society at all levels: the level of ordinary family networks, of local schooling, of ordinary housing and the ordinary workplace, among other things. The more we continue to separate people from everyday experiences and opportunities within society, the more we disempower them. Services which support and harness the power of natural networks, use person centred approaches, operate as open rather than closed organisations and put the interests of service users before those of the organisation are bound to be more empowering than those which don't. The more we facilitate inclusion, the closer we move towards empowerment. The crucial question is: How should we be doing this?

Being excluded – a conversation with Jimmy

J   I think it's a big disadvantage when people make fun of you and laugh at you, especially if you're going out to buy something and they tend to laugh at you and make jokes and that.

Q   *Does that happen to you?*

J   That's happened a few times.

Q   *Tell me what happened.*

J   I went up to the building place, and I said to the guy, 'How much is top soil?', and he just laughed at me and said, '£400'.

Q   *What did you do?*

J   I couldn't do anything – I just felt that small.

Q   *Did you say anything to him?*

J   I couldn't.

Q   *So what did you do then?*

J   I just walked away.

Q   *Why couldn't you do anything?*

J   I was that ashamed – you see, well, when I was in the hospital, I was only told one rule, and it got drummed into me – shut up and listen. I got told that many times, so I find it difficult to say anything to anybody. I still do.

Q   *Why?*

J   Because I've had it drummed into me that many times that long.

Q   *And do you think that was right to be told to shut up?*

J   No.

Q   *Why not?*

J   I think I should have been able to speak up for myself.

Q   *And how about now? Can you speak up for yourself now?*

J   No.

Q   *What do you think might help you to speak up for yourself?*

J   I haven't a clue. I haven't forgotten the first time I went down to the buroo [employment office] – when I went to see the buroo about employment the woman didn't even look at me. She just kept on writing and ignoring me.

Q   *What did you do?*

J   I couldn't do anything about that.

Q   *How did you feel, though, that stopped you doing anything?*

J   I felt like I was in a room on my own and couldn't get out.

Q   *And how did that make you feel?*

J   I felt useless.

Q   *And how about now?*

J   I'm not bad now. I can make my own decisions and that, but I like help to be able to speak up and that.

Q   *What's helped you to make your own decisions?*

J   I started to feel a change about two years ago. That's when I decided I'm more independent. I won't let anybody tell me how to run my life – what I can do and what I can't do.

You'll have heard it said that *information is power.* Access to information enables us to learn about our rights within society, make complaints, understand how society operates, find out about services available to us, add to our own knowledge, contact people – and a whole host of other things. Conversely, exclusion from information we need and have a right to has the opposite effect. People with learning disabilities are, we know, often excluded because of *the way information is presented and accessed* – inaccessible language, written or verbal, lack of access to the right people, not knowing how or where to access relevant information or having the support or means to do so, and so on. Many support services or related groups have taken on the challenge of overcoming this. Perhaps yours is one of them.

Reflection

In your service, how is information made more accessible to service users and to families? How does this contribute to empowerment?

Are there any aspects of the service that prevent service users or families getting access to information they should have? How does this disempower them?

What about *involvement* as empowerment? Or perhaps *active participation* is a better description. I'm never fully satisfied with any of these terms, nor with *partnership* – all have their drawbacks, but you'll know what I mean. I'm talking about people with learning disabilities taking on roles which have traditionally been denied them and which have been the domain of the 'professionals' (perhaps there's a link with normalisation here?). This type of active participation happens through:

- being partners in research

- being partners in policy-making

- being on staff selection and interview panels

- working as trainers

- taking a full and equal part in planning services and quality monitoring

- campaigning for your rights

- exploring your own life history and having other people acknowledge it

- having control over your own life through such things as direct payments, and being involved in service design and staff selection

- through self-advocacy (discussed on page 55)

This list is not exhaustive by any means, but it's a start – you'll be able to add to it from your own experience. Perhaps you have an example from your own service – the next activity is about this.

ACTIVITY 5: **Empowerment in practice**

The idea in this activity is to explore staff perceptions of how empowerment is happening in your own service, then service users' perceptions and then compare the two.

To do this, prepare a few questions (about 4 or 5) which you can use with staff to find out how they believe the service is helping users to become empowered. Next time you have a few staff members together (at a staff meeting, for example) ask these questions and see what people think.

If there isn't an occasion to speak to people in a group, ask a few individually.

Now adapt your questions to get the same information from service users and compare their answers to those of the staff.

If you work with people who don't communicate verbally you can ask family carers, advocates and befrienders, and use your observation skills, to see if these sources confirm staff opinions.

Comment

How did you get on? Did you have to adapt this activity? The word 'empowerment' probably wouldn't be familiar to some service users so you have to have expressed it differently (I found this when I asked some people). Empowerment may be one of the principle objectives of your service and may be written in documents, but things that are written don't always happen, or they happen in ways we're not aware of. You may not have had occasion to explore empowerment explicitly. You may find from this activity that people can suggest other things the service can do, or change, to promote empowerment further.

How Lily's life changed

Ever since I moved to [current service] we've got a lot of tenant's rights – more than what I had in children's homes and hostels. I think what's made me more confident is that I was involved a lot in the tenants' advisory group. I did the induction course and the foundation course which meant that if there were any new projects opening up, myself and someone else from the tenants' advisory group would go along to the new project and just talk to the new folk who would be starting to work with [the service] to tell them how to treat people with either a learning, physical, multiple or mental health disability.

The foundation course – I did that up at head office because that was for the likes of folks who have worked in [the service] for about three or four years, just to update them in *The same as you?* learning disability regime. Because that's all we're asking – for people to be treated the same as anybody else. That built up my confidence because when I was in [previous service] – if you had known me about eleven years ago I wouldn't even have sat here and spoken to you because I just didn't have the confidence.

Well, like, I'm a volunteer for Sense in Scotland, in [street]. That's a charity shop. When I first started in the shop I was scared to tell the boss that I had epilepsy, and someone that used to work there said, 'You're going to have to tell them at some point, because what will happen if you have a seizure? They will think you've been out on the ran-dan the night before.' So what I did was told the boss and she says, 'So what of it? You have epilepsy. You've told us that as a precautionary measure. There will be no discrimination in here, because you'll get treated the same. You'll just be treated the same as paid employees, by Sense.'

Advocacy

The British Institute of Learning Disabilities (BILD), which is responsible for managing the central government Citizen Advocacy Funding Programme (described in Valuing People), identifies four types of advocacy in relation to people with learning disabilities: self-advocacy, peer advocacy, paid independent or professional advocacy and citizen advocacy. The two which have become most commonly known are self-advocacy and citizen advocacy.

McNally (2003, p.504) describes advocacy as 'the process of speaking out or acting on behalf of another person who is unable to do so for himself' (or, presumably, herself) and also as 'a process by which service users, individually or in groups, make service providers aware of their views and interests (Monarch and Spriggs, 1994)'.

The Scottish Independent Advocacy Alliance identifies the following main purposes of advocacy:

- safeguarding people who are vulnerable and discriminated against or whom services find difficult to serve

- empowering people who need a stronger voice by enabling them to express their own needs and make their own decisions

- enabling people to gain access to information, explore and understand their options, and make their views and wishes known

- speaking on behalf of people who are unable to do so for themselves (www.theadvocacyproject.org.uk)

Advocacy is not new to people with learning disabilities, but until now its development has been patchy. With the advent of *The same as you?* and *Valuing People*, advocacy has been officially recognised as the powerful force for change it really is and efforts are being made to support its current and future development.

Valuing People says: 'Effective advocacy can transform the lives of people with learning disabilities by enabling them to express their wishes and aspirations and make real choices ... With the right support, many people with learning disabilities can become effective self-advocates. The growth of the self-advocacy movement shows how people with learning disabilities can make a real difference to service development and delivery. Citizen advocates make a vital contribution to enabling the voices of people with more complex disabilities to be heard' (p. 46).

And from *The same as you?*: 'Many people with learning disabilities want to be able to speak up for themselves. They would like to be trained to represent themselves or others ... Advocacy needs to be more widely available. We need to build towards a position where everyone who has complex needs or is particularly vulnerable has ready access to an advocate' (p.36).

Bersani (1998) charts the development of the self-advocacy movement, identifying the following 'landmarks':

- its origins in social clubs in Sweden (1965) for people with learning disabilities, linked to normalisation

- sports clubs in Denmark which became 'culture conferences' providing opportunities to study democracy and which ultimately became self-advocacy activities

- the development of social clubs in Massachusetts, USA, whose members became interested in social issues

- the efforts of a small group of people with learning disabilities in Oregon, USA, credited in 1973 with formulating the statement, 'We are people first'

Today, self-advocacy in the UK is best known through the coalition of groups under the auspices of the People First movement.

Four types of self-advocacy groups have been identified in literature:

- the autonomous or ideal model, independent from professional or parent groups

- the divisional model, formed as part of an existing parent or professional organisation

- the coalition model, which brings together people with different types of disabilities

- the service-based model, based in a service setting

The autonomous group is the most empowering and the service-based group has been the most heavily criticised. Downer and Ferns (1993) have tried to resolve the tension between services and self-advocacy by stressing the importance of self-advocacy in day and residential services, but highlighting the importance of the groups' rights to autonomy (McNally, 2003). This has particular significance for the current discussion.

Self-advocacy and citizen advocacy, if taken seriously, have considerable implications for service development, including:

- stronger voices for service users in service planning, service delivery and quality assurance

- a clearer role for service users

- the possibility of real change which benefits everyone

- capacity building for staff and service users

- better opportunities for the service to contribute to regional and local developments

In England advocacy is a priority area for the Department of Health Learning Disability Development Fund. People from black and minority ethnic communities are mentioned particularly, since they find it particularly difficult to access advocacy services.

You might like to read. . .

Innovations in Advocacy and Empowerment for People with Intellectual Disabilities
edited by Linda Ward (1998) Lisieux Hall Publications, Chorley

---

Some services have changed radically because of self-advocacy and changes in ideas and understanding by both service providers and users. Perhaps yours is one of these, or perhaps this has happened to a service you know. Such changes are challenging for everyone and staff resistance can be one of the biggest problems for managers.

ACTIVITY 6: **The effects of advocacy on service development**

Think of a situation known to you which involved either citizen advocacy or self-advocacy. Did any of the following changes result from this?:

	Yes	No	Not sure
● More meaningful involvement for service users in planning and service development	Yes	No	Not sure
● Changes in the hours of the service	Yes	No	Not sure
● Changes in staff responsibilities	Yes	No	Not sure
● Greater involvement for service users in staff selection and appointment	Yes	No	Not sure
● A move from larger to smaller premises	Yes	No	Not sure
● Greater diversification in the role of the service	Yes	No	Not sure
● Changes in the policies of the service	Yes	No	Not sure
● A reduction in the number of people using the service	Yes	No	Not sure

Choose two of these changes, or two changes not mentioned, and describe the role of advocacy or self-advocacy in bringing them about.

Comment

I don't know, of course, what your answers are. Advocacy *should* be making a difference to your service. If it isn't, you might like to reflect on the reasons for this. If it is, is this something that could be useful for others to know about? Could you write it up for a journal (in partnership with service users, of course) or for a website, or find another way of disseminating it? You might also like to reflect on the reasons for its impact.

Social inclusion

Social inclusion is identified as a key principle in *Valuing People* (DoH, 2001) and *The same as you?* (Scottish Executive, 2000). Like empowerment, social inclusion can be invested with a wide range of meanings, depending on whether we adopt a sociological, structural or political stance. At the root of social inclusion is the need to change systems and structures which bring about the exclusion of all oppressed groups within society, which includes people with learning disabilities.

Social inclusion means people being able to:

- participate in, benefit from and contribute to society

- claim their full human and citizenship rights

- access the same opportunities and use the same facilities as other people for education, housing, employment, health and leisure and having the support which will enable you to do this

A comment from Lily

The doctor that I am under, he's all for people with a learning, physical, multiple or mental health disability – he often says the same as me – don't look at the person's disability, you look at them as individuals and the ability that each of them has got.

Atherton (2003) makes the following important points about social inclusion:

- Despite the closure of most long-stay institutions, the extent of social inclusion is debatable.

- Material and physical advances, such as ordinary housing, have been much easier to achieve than involvement in community networks which facilitate friendships and relationships, and valued social roles and status.

- Services remain, on the whole, large scale and segregated.

- Fewer than 10% of people are in employment.

- Social inclusion is much harder to achieve for people with profound and multiple disabilities and those from black and minority ethnic communities.

- It would appear that people with learning disabilities are still among the least accepted disabled groups in society.

- There is some evidence that eugenic attitudes continue to exist but in socially acceptable guises.

> 'There is now an acceptance by social researchers that not only must research elicit the views of people with learning difficulties, but that credence must be given to these views. Participatory methodology enables people with learning difficulties to work in partnership with researchers and have greater influence over the processes of research, an opportunity which has been denied them hitherto. It has provided greater opportunities for people with learning difficulties to engage with the research process and influence the way in which their experiences are conveyed via the research.' (Chappell, 2000, p.42)

Walsh (1997), writing about European perspectives on learning disability, recommends the strategies of subversion of national administrations (eg asking awkward questions and providing awkward data), collaboration (with social partners, architects of services systems, holders of the public purse) and discovery (recreating ourselves by learning from the inclusion of disabled people) to help us achieve inclusive societies. She says: 'An inclusive vision compels us to extend human rights to every citizen, to set worthy goals and to shape the social policies which pursue these goals. A striving for integration, the embrace of diversity, the solidarity achieved through shared effort: these reflect a European tradition which is at once the brightest hope for its own future and its best gift to the other countries of the world' (p.117).

Legislation, policy and service development

You are bound to be more familiar with some legislation and policy developments than others, according to the nature of the service you work for and which country of the UK you live in. I've listed some of the key Acts and documents below. You can get more information from the following websites:

- www.doh.gov.uk/learningdisabilities
- www.scotland.gov.uk/ldsr
- www.wales.gov.uk

Legislation

Legislation in the UK is complicated by the fact that there are some differences between England (E), Scotland (S), Wales (W) and Northern Ireland (NI). Here are some of the key pieces of legislation, some of which apply to the UK in general and some to specific countries:

- Data Protection Act 1984
- NHS and Community Care Act 1990 (E, W and S)
- Health and Personal Social Services (Northern Ireland) Order 1991
- Disability Discrimination Act 1995
- Human Rights Act 1998
- Community Care (Direct Payments) Act 1996 (E, W and S)
- Care Standards Act 2000
- Adults with Incapacity (Scotland) Act 2000
- Regulation of Care (Scotland) Act 2001
- Community Care and Health (Scotland) Act 2002
- NHS Reform and Health Care Professions Act – Health and Well-being Strategies (Wales) Regulations 2002/03

Policy documents and developments

- *No Secrets* Guidance on Developing Multi-Agency Policies and Procedures to Protect Vulnerable Adults from Abuse

- Establishment of the General Social Services Council and Social Services Council in Scotland, Wales and Northern Ireland to the Scottish Social Services Council (SSSC) to regulate the social service workforce and their education and training, publish codes of practice

- Guidebook for Purchasers and Providers of Learning Disability Services (DoH, 1996)

- The Codes of Practice for social care employers and workers which lay down standards of conduct and practice

Appendix 6 of *The same as you?* sets out the legal background for services, which is particularly useful. If you don't have a copy of this document you can access it at: www.scotland.gov.uk/idsr/docs/tsay-11.asp

---

ACTIVITY 7: **Changing policy – changing services**

For this activity you need a copy of *The same as you?* or *Valuing People* or *Fulfilling the Promise*, whichever document is relevant to your service.

Spend some time reading through the document, making notes on issues that are particularly relevant to your own service and identifying key headings.

Now imagine what your service will look like in five years' time if it is to begin to realise the objectives in the document. Write a short report describing this service of the future.

Use your key headings as a structure for the report.

Identify areas of major change such as resources, staff recruitment, staff mix and training at all service levels.

Conclude your report with recommendations for action now and over the next five years.

Comment

The plans for the support services of people with learning disabilities in the UK mean considerable change for most services: a much stronger voice for service users and families, much more use of mainstream services, fewer segregated services and so on. You might like to reflect on the challenges this will bring, as well as the rewards.

Concluding comment

Empowerment, advocacy and social inclusion are key concepts in services for people with learning disabilities but are often easier to talk about than to put into practice. However, we're learning! The increasing use of the internet means that information about, and examples of, good practice are easier to access than they ever were. In the resources section of this book you will find some websites you might find useful.

It is important also for services which aren't so well known or publicised to contribute to the development of knowledge and good practice, something which can most effectively be done through networking, as discussed in chapter 6. Are there things happening in your service in relation to advocacy, empowerment and inclusion which would be useful to other services? How could you disseminate this information?

In the next chapter, the focus is person centred planning. Or should it be person centred *practice* – including not only planning and approaches, but all we do in our professional activities?

Chapter 4

Person centred planning

Introduction

Person centred planning is a fundamentally different way of seeing and working with people with disabilities. Being 'person centred' or using a 'person centred approach' means ensuring that everything we do is based upon what is important to a person from their own perspective. Person centred planning discovers and acts on what is important to a person.

Person centred planning helps us do this by discovering and acting on what matters to a person. It gives us a structure to help us continually listen and learn about what is important to a person now and in the future and to act on this in alliance with friends and family. It requires a fundamental shift of thinking from a 'power over' relationship to a 'power with' relationship.

(BILD Factsheet by Charlotte Sweeney and Helen Sanderson, February 2002)

The journey from institutionalisation towards justice, equality and respect for people with learning disabilities has been marked in recent times by one of the most significant developments in the provision of support services – person centred planning (PCP). In this chapter I discuss:

- the basic principles of person centred planning

- the process of person centred planning

- the differences between person centred planning and other approaches

- the systems and structures which enable the users of services to be central to, and in control of, their own support plans

- the information systems needed to support the process of person centred planning

- the process of person centred planning in relation to review and evaluation

- barriers or obstacles to person centred planning

There has been a great deal written about person centred planning, both in the UK and internationally. My intention in this chapter is not to provide an exhaustive account of person centred planning – probably an impossible task anyway – but to focus instead on the importance of person centred planning in the development of support services. In the resources section of this book I list a number of references that will enable you to obtain further information about aspects of PCP you wish to explore in more depth.

The basic principles of person centred planning

Person centred planning emerged from the philosophies, practices and ideas discussed in chapter 1, which attempted to right the wrongs of the oppression, segregation and incarceration of large numbers of people with learning disabilities. Its roots are in normalisation, social role valorisation, individual planning and the ordinary life movement, which were professional initiatives, but also in self-advocacy and the social model of disability (discussed in chapter 5). Person centred planning has clear links with social inclusion.

Sanderson (2003) says: 'Person centred planning is a process of continual listening and learning, focused on what is important to someone with learning disabilities now, and for the future, and acting on this in alliance with the person's family and friends. There is a family of approaches to person centred planning. These approaches share common values and principles, and are used to answer two fundamental questions:

- Who are you, and who are we in your life?

- What can we do together to achieve a better life for you now, and in the future?' (p.370)

This question of 'who are we in your life?', particularly, is a radical departure from traditional approaches, where there have generally been predetermined roles for professionals, often to the exclusion of a person's family members or friends.

The basic principles of person centred planning are:

- a commitment to shared power and the empowerment of people with learning disabilities, particularly important since people with learning disabilities are usually in disempowered and disempowering situations

- the rights of every person to self-determination and control over his or her own life, to independence and individual choice, and to social inclusion

Sanderson (2003) identifies five key features of person centred planning:

- The person is at the centre.

- Family members and friends are partners in planning.

- The plan reflects: what is important to the person; his or her capacities; the support he or she requires.

- The plan results in actions that are about life, not about services, and reflects what is possible, not just what is available.

- Ongoing listening, learning and further action are integral parts of the process.

The process of person centred planning

Person centred planning involves a number of steps:

- the person concerned bringing together the people he or she wants to be involved, or someone close (an advocate) doing this if the person cannot do this him or herself

- the person, or advocate, choosing a facilitator, then selecting the most appropriate 'tools' (planning styles or devices) for the process

- the use of a series of questions to obtain salient information which will help all concerned to understand the person and his or her situation

- decisions being taken and a plan being drawn up, specifying the supports required

- implementing the plan, monitoring and evaluating progress

The process continues, with the necessary adaptations as progress is made.

Sanderson (2000) describes person centred planning as a 'family of approaches' and says: 'It is not simply a collection of new techniques for planning to replace individual programme planning. It is based on a completely different way of seeing and working with people with disabilities, which is fundamentally about sharing power and community inclusion'.

There are several ways of doing person centred planning, usually referred to as planning 'styles'. These include:

- *Essential lifestyle planning* (Smull and Burke-Harrison in Sanderson, 2000) which is an extremely detailed planning style; the focus is the person's life now and what can be improved, what is important to the person and what support is required for him or her to have a good quality of life from the person's own perspective

- *PATH (Planning Alternative Tomorrows with Hope)* (Pearpoint, Forest and O'Brien, 1993), which has a strong focus on a desirable future or dream and what it would take to move closer to that; planning is based on direct and immediate action

- *Personal futures planning* (Mount, 1990), in which a committed group of people describe the person's life now and help the person move towards his or her desirable future; this style helps others learn more about the person's life and create a vision for the future, building on areas that are working well

- *MAPs (Making Action Plans)* (Snow, Pearpoint and Forest in Sanderson, 2000) in which the focus is on 'who is the person?' and 'what are his or her gifts?'; the process includes the person's history and enables the person to express both hopes (dreams) and fears (nightmares) for the future; the action plan involves moving towards dream and away from nightmare

Each planning style involves:

- a series of questions for getting to understand the person and his or her situation

- a particular process for engaging people

- bringing all contributions together,

- making decisions

- a distinctive role for facilitator(s)

(Sanderson, 2000)

You might like to read . . .

'Person centred planning' by Helen Sanderson in Gates, B (ed) (2003) *Learning Disabilities: Toward Inclusion*, London, Churchill Livingstone

People, Plans and Possibilities – Exploring Person Centred Planning (2002) by Helen Sanderson, Jo Kennedy, Pete Ritchie and Gill Goodwin. Available from Scottish Human Services (tel: 0131 538 7717)

The differences between person centred planning and other approaches

Person centred planning can be seen as a set of techniques within the wider context of person centred approaches, but there is a world of difference between person centred planning and the approaches we have been accustomed to. Traditional approaches to planning were determined by professionals and based on the philosophy and practices of the particular profession involved. For people with learning disabilities these had a strong medical bias. People were defined in terms of deficiencies which needed to be remedied, thus intervention was designed to make up the deficits so that people could fit into existing services.

Person centred planning has changed all that. It was influenced by dissatisfaction with individual programme planning (IPP) which 'required that staff behaved in a synchronised and standardised way. Person centred planning requires that staff have a flexible and responsive approach to meet peoples' changing circumstances, guided by the principles of good planning rather than a standard procedure. Staff need to be constantly problem solving in partnership with the person and their family and friends' (Sanderson, 2000).

There are fundamental differences between person centred planning and other approaches, including:

- The person with learning disability, not the professionals, is recognised as the 'expert'.

- The process involves shared problem solving, not decision-making by professionals which takes the decision-making out of the hands of the person concerned.

- The professional role is different: it is that of a partner with a particular contribution to offer in terms of particular skills, knowledge and experience which can enable the person to achieve his or her desired lifestyle. Sanderson (2000) calls them 'backstage technicians', which brings to mind a well-known slogan from the social model of disability: 'Professionals should be on tap, not on top'.

- The process is likely to involve professionals other than the traditional ones such as social workers, doctors, nurses and psychologists; depending on the person's circumstances and aspirations, these could include 'mainstream' professionals such as lawyers, housing specialists and financial advisors, for example.

- Family members and friends play a much more significant role – they are partners in the process.

- Person centred planning is not in the control of statutory authorities and there are no professional hierarchies.

One of the hallmarks of person centred planning is its flexibly and inventiveness. The process acknowledges the uniqueness of the individual and brings together all the key people in that person's life as equal partners (Styring, 2003).

Traditional approaches to planning are inseparable from service systems and structures. They have constrained possibilities and opportunities since they generally have taken account only of what is already available, often because of resources limitations. Since the vast majority of services for people with learning disabilities are segregated, they do not reflect everyday life. Efforts to move beyond the segregated system and into mainstream society are inevitably challenging because they involve cohesion between two institutions that are fundamentally different philosophically and in practice. People with learning disabilities are stigmatised not only because of being labelled 'different' but also because they are associated with institutions for people who have to be segregated on account of this difference. Person centred planning is more compatible with social inclusion than any other planning approach because it starts from a premise of equality, control over your own life and the right to exercise choice, make your own decisions and use naturally occurring networks. It also removes the hierarchical gaps between professionals and 'others'.

Sweeney and Sanderson (2002) stress that person centred planning is not:

- the same as assessment and care planning

- only for people who are 'easy to work with'

- an end in itself, but a powerful tool in enabling people to get the lives they want

- a replacement for other necessary forms of planning (but other planning should take account of person centred principles)

Service ethos, systems and structures which facilitate control by service users

Undoubtedly, person centred planning presents us with significant challenges, not only to our way of thinking but also to established systems, structures and practices. Sanderson (2000) makes an interesting point when she says, 'Some people believe that service systems will inevitably pervert the possibilities of person centred planning and choose to work at the very edge of the service system, encouraging people to get out of, or avoid moving into the system. Some of the founders of different styles of person centred planning would be very concerned if a service tried to adopt that style of planning through a service (eg John O'Brien, Beth Mount). They believe that person centred planning should focus on those people who now get least from the system – those living with family members. They see person centred planning as a powerful support to families with disabled members at home and believe that focusing person centred planning on people already in some kind of residential service is another case of ignoring the many people who have only a little share of system resources.'

All services have a responsibility to adopt person centred planning and many have already done so. There are now more people with learning disabilities in their own homes, in jobs and in mainstream adult and continuing education settings. More people are getting married and having their own families. Hospital closures are continuing, though it remains to be seen whether some people will end up in what are often described as 'mini-institutions'. Many day centres have decentralised their services and some act only as points of contact or administration. There are more and more services without buildings. More children are attending mainstream schools and inclusive education is government policy, although there are various loopholes.

Certain systems, structures and practices are more conducive to person centred planning than others. In particular:

'Open' rather than 'closed' services

Support services and facilities which are located within the community, are part of the community and are built upon community networks and resources, and which have inclusion as their goal, are in the best position to implement person centred planning. Conversely, services which are removed from the community, either philosophically or geographically, and in which the interests of the organisation take precedence will have far greater challenges. For them, person centred planning will entail substantial shifts in ideology and working practices.

New opportunities, not existing services

Person centred planning enables people to harness new opportunities – and strengthen existing positive experiences – that will both enrich their lives and lead to social inclusion, with the necessary network of support. Thus support services need to have social inclusion as their goal, flexible ways of working, problem solving and partnership approaches, as well as capacity building opportunities for service users, staff and families.

Involvement in all aspects of service planning and development

Person centred planning also means having a service ethos that respects and recognises service users as equal partners in all aspects of the service: planning and design; commissioning; staff selection and training; monitoring, evaluation and ongoing development and change.

Service ethos

Person centred planning flourishes in services in which respect for individuality, diversity (ability, gender, ethnic background, age, sexual orientation) and personal aspiration are paramount, where there is an openness to learning from service users and families and a shared commitment to learning together. Such services need support workers and managers who are:

- good listeners
- equipped with good observation skills and facilitative and sensitive questioning skills
- able to understand another person's perspective
- able to absorb information and to present information in alternative ways, eg signs and symbols
- able to relate to a variety of people

- good with recording skills

- skilled in identifying and obtaining resources and helping people to make connections

Putting service users at the centre and in control of their own plans

Support workers and managers can ensure that service users are at the centre by:

- recognising that the person is in charge; adopting working practices that empower and do not demoralise

- seeing that the aspirations, opinions, hopes and preferences are truly those of the person concerned

- upholding the person's rights

Process as well as outcome is important; the person should be in control and take the lead. The person concerned should be consulted throughout the planning process, choose who to involve in the process and choose the setting and timing of meetings (Sanderson, 2003).

Information systems which support person centred planning

If they are to support person centred planning, services must establish systems which make information available and accessible to all service users and family members as well as staff and managers. This means:

- providing information in appropriate forms, eg using alternative or augmentative communication approaches such as pictures, signing and symbols; audio tapes or visual aids

- using plain English and avoiding jargon

- presenting information in relevant languages and in appropriate cultural formats, as well as ensuring access to this information through appropriate channels, eg not using children as the main channel of communication because parents might not understand English; investigating alternative ways of making information accessible for different cultural communities

- using a range of methods for record keeping, eg large print or pictorial records such as diaries, photographs, videos

- making sure that service users and families are familiar with communication systems, lines of accountability and responsibility, information storage, complaints procedures and similar information systems and know how to use them

- ensuring that service users and families are aware of confidentiality policies and involving them in the development of these and similar policies

- involving service users and their families in the design and development of information systems

Some comments from families about services

What we expect of services

'that they can meet our need'

'that they will deliver what they promise or agree'

'to listen to my needs and communicate about plans and changes'

'partnership working with the focus on my daughter but acknowledging our family's expertise, knowledge and role in making it successful for her'

'that they can do what we want them to'

The problems we face in using services

'lack of communication'

'The service isn't what we asked for, and now we can't change it.'

'If I complain about this worker, I will lose the whole service.'

'The service is not flexible enough to give us exactly what we want, so that we have to fit around what we are offered, or get nothing at all.'

'inconsistency – not getting the same support worker/s regularly; information isn't passed between old and new workers'

'The workers and the manager say they are being person centred by listening to my son, rather than family members, but I feel he has been led, persuaded, etc by the staff.'

'If the family doesn't push for a review things will carry on with no change.'

'no communication or understanding between a number of services for [my daughter] and lack of co-ordination between them'

'It's difficult to understanding who provides which service, how they link, which are social work or voluntary or...'

Person centred planning, monitoring, reviewing and evaluating services

The most robust and reliable type of evaluation is that which is undertaken by the people central to any situation. I would not ask or allow you to evaluate the quality of my life, nor would you permit me to do this for you. So why should we think we can do it for people with learning disabilities? Person centred planning is invaluable not only for planning and subsequent action, but also for monitoring, review and evaluation. It embodies the essentials of participatory evaluation and has emerged from the same roots of social justice and inclusion.

There are many explanations of participatory evaluation, but the one I like best for our purposes is:

> 'One of the negative connotations often associated with evaluation is that it is something done to people. One is evaluated. Participatory evaluation, in contrast, is a process controlled by the people in the program or community. It is something they undertake as a formal, reflective process for their own development and empowerment.'
> (M. Patton, 1990, p 129)

Person centred planning encompasses monitoring, review and evaluation, because:

- The aim of PCP is social inclusion and the use of community indicators to assess progress.

- PCP facilitates ongoing capacity building, based on feedback of progress, which in turn leads to improvement, as monitoring and evaluation should.

- Opportunities for reflection, analysis and subsequent action are part of the process – these are aspects of monitoring, review and evaluation.

- The lessons learned are used for further development, a requirement of monitoring, review and evaluation.

- Change is more likely as a result of PCP, because of the inherent process of reflection and discussion.

- The continual information feedback and the participatory nature of the process of PCP lead to corrective actions and improvements, which is the goal of monitoring, review and evaluation.

The process and its lessons can be considered both in relation to an individual service user and to the service as a whole. Feedback from the planning and implementation processes at individual level can help a service (and its allies) improve its systems and structures, develop its networks by making new connections and find more creative ways of supporting people. The fact that service users and families are involved in monitoring, review and evaluation at both individual and service level will ensure that development maintains a person centred focus.

Barriers or obstacles to person centred planning

Services based on the social model of disability, which we will discuss in the next chapter, recognise that among the problems people with learning disabilities face are the barriers and obstacles which are put up against their social inclusion and control of their own lives. There are a number of barriers or obstacles to effective person centred planning which may be encountered:

- staff attitudes, which we have discussed earlier in this chapter – negative approaches build barriers, but positive ones dismantle them

- resources – person centred planning takes not only a great deal of staff input, but a lot of time

- structure of organisations – for example some service providers do not have the type of financial or quality control arrangements needed

---

ACTIVITY 8: **Finding out more about person centred planning**

There is a great deal of information about person centred planning on the internet. Choose two of the websites listed at the end of this reader and log on to them. Make a list of the key points and think about how these relate to your service.

Concluding comments

I'll leave the last word on this chapter to some mothers commenting about person centred practice for their sons and daughters (Sanderson et al, 2002).

'Person centred planning enables you to dream without denying the person's support needs and gives hope for a wonderful future.' (Lynne, Nicola's Mum)

'I know Sophie best. I am the expert in her life. Person centred planning helped me to know that what I was thinking was right.' (Julia, Sophie's Mum)

'Through person centred planning we see Martin for the wonderful character he is, not the labels they give him. It has given our family an understanding of what is important to him so he can be himself, and what support he needs to achieve his aspirations.' (Margaret, Martin's Mum)

'There are so many reviews, reports and everything else that they put together about your child. They do not talk about the person, their character, their gifts or anything like that. I had never been asked what I liked about my child until I did person centred planning.' (Joan, Layla's Mum)

'Person centred planning has given us hope and a vision for a better future for Mohammed. We feel now we can have a say in how and what service support he receives. We no longer believe that only professionals know best for our son. Mohammed's faith and cultural needs are recognised and responded to.' (Joynab, Mohammed's mother)

'Discovering person centred planning and circles of support was wonderful – we got our daughter back. She has become more confident and always been at the centre of her plans, which feels like celebrations of her and lifts all our spirits. Nicola's circle of support has helped us to develop an Essential Lifestyle Plan (an approach to person centred planning) with Nicola. This means that lots more people can spend time with her and be confident when supporting her. As her mother it has made me feel much happier knowing that the people with her have detailed information about everything they need to know when with Nicola. We then went on to do a MAP (another approach to person centred planning) with Nicola and her 'circle' for the first time in years we felt we could dream with Nicola about her future, face our nightmares. It was a joy to hear people talking about the Nicola they know, not a list of labels and needs.' (Lynne, Nicola's Mum)

Chapter 5

Models of disability and their effects on service development

Introduction

I recently watched one of those television programmes that show advertisements from other countries and from British archives which have audiences in gales of laughter. One, from the 1950s, features a trim, well-groomed woman wearing a pretty and pristine apron and ironing her husband's shirts, and extols the virtues of a particular brand of washing machine, showing how it enables the woman to get all the housework done, the children clean and presentable and the dinner on the table while still looking her best, all ready for her husband when he arrives home – tired and in need of pampering – from his important job of work. Such an advertisement would cause outrage today (even if there are still people who believe a woman's place is in the kitchen!). Society has changed, significantly.

These changes have had no less impact for people with learning disabilities than for the rest of us – maybe even more, if we think back through history. In this respect, one of the most promising debates, I believe, is that around the social construction of disability. Promising because its resolution demands radical reform within society – nothing incremental here! Promising also because the significance of the social model of disability for people with learning disabilities has only just begun to be explored. Promising because of the potential for closing the gap between the disability movement as a whole in the UK and people with learning disabilities. And, not least, promising because of the possibilities of the social model for people with learning disabilities, and the challenges it presents, both to them and to the rest of us. These issues are the focus of this chapter. In particular:

- the social construction of disability and the move towards a more balanced view of the role of the medical model

- the relevance of the social model of disability for people with learning disabilities

- the advantages and disadvantages of knowing the causes of a learning disability and the possible physical, cognitive and behavioural effects of a particular syndrome or condition

- the features of services which are based on a social model of disability

History shows clearly how disability became increasingly medicalised, giving rise to what we now refer to as the 'medical model' of disability. Finklestein and Stuart (1996) identify key points in this process:

- The medical model gained its importance not through the supremacy of this approach over other models but organically over a long historical period of neglect.

- In this way the medical profession gained dominance over the services administered to disabled people.

- Medical interpretations of disability have been given outstanding prominence in the administration of interventions to cater for 'the incapable disabled'.

The medical model of disability

The key faults of the medical model of disability are that:

- 'Disability' is regarded as individual pathology – in other words, the problem lies with the person and any difficulties are the result of the impairment. Oliver (1996) calls this 'personal tragedy theory'.

- The focus is on the person's impairment – he or she is defined by the impairment to the disregard of anything else, including common humanity.

- The person is perceived as unable to fit into, or play the required part in, society and viewed as unproductive socially and economically.

- The person is seen as helpless, dependent, 'unfortunate, useless, different, oppressed and sick' (Hunt 1966) and poses 'a direct challenge to commonly held western values' (Barnes, 1997).

When disabled people are defined by their impairment:

- There is an acceptance that others have the right to identify their 'deficits' and make decisions for them – hence assessment focusing on deficits, special and prescriptive 'programmes' to remedy the deficit, and similar practices.

- They experience stigma, stereotyping, discrimination, rejection and separation from mainstream society – hence institutions, special schools, barriers to work and so on; in other words, they are marked out as different and experience social oppression.

- They are at the mercy of 'a multitude of professionals and services to enable them to come to terms with their impairments, rehabilitate them into non-disabled society or remove them from it (if they cannot be "cured")' (Chappell et al, 2001).

Rioux (1997) identifies two approaches that result from the perception of disability as individual pathology. The first, the bio-medical approach, illustrates 'the extent to which medical science took over control of disability: Assessments became a scientifically justified activity extending to various aspects of an individual's range of disability such as educational, training and work capabilities; fine motor skills and hand–eye co-ordination; the need for financial benefits and mobility aids and devices; as well as access to rehabilitation' (p.105). The second, the functional approach, considers that people have functional incapacity as a result of their impairment, so services are made available to help them become as socially functional as possible. Success is measured by how closely they 'can approximate to the lives of "normal people" and "achieve the skills of non-disabled persons"'(p.105).

Another part of Lily's story

Then when I was in the hostel we had to be in for like half past nine every night. We didn't have any privacy – there were about four or five of us sharing the one bedroom – no privacy at all. If we wanted to go out we had to be back in the hostel by half past nine every night. If we weren't back by half past nine they phoned the police. You just didn't have a say – like you had to be in your bed for about half ten, eleven o'clock, no say – and we weren't allowed to cash our own pension books. It was done, like, automatically for us.

Somebody that used to work in the hostel with me, she said to me, 'How about writing a life story, maybe putting a couple of photographs in and we could send it to some organisation' – no, it wasn't in the hostel, it was in the children's home – but I didn't really know my parents. Like when they came to visit me for the first time with the social worker, the social worker introduced me to my parents, and I said I don't have a mother or a father, that's my mother there ... because I hadn't seen them in years – how was I to know I had any parents?

The role of the medical model

The medical model should not be confused with the *health and well-being model* on which our medical services are based and which applies to everyone, including people with learning disabilities. The medical model is about social control on the basis of impairment whereas the health and well-being model is about having access to appropriate health services. There is a considerable amount of research which shows that people with learning disabilities do not have equal access to health service support, for a variety of reasons, so this is something which needs to be addressed urgently, bearing in mind the following points:

- the evidence that people with a learning disability encounter more illness than the general population but make less use of medical services

- indications that as a result of this there exists a high level of unmet medical need among people who have learning disabilities

- that some conditions, for example Down syndrome, can cause not only learning disabilities but also a characteristic pattern of health problems for which help is available

- that some genetic conditions are associated with both learning disability and certain patterns of behaviour or behavioural phenotypes which may require support, for example Tourette syndrome

The social model of disability

An alternative approach to understanding disability originated in the UK in the mid-1970s with the Union of the Physically Impaired Against Segregation (UPIAS). Oliver (1983) deemed this a 'social model of disability'. 'The social model distinguishes between impairment (ie the loss or lack of some functioning part of the body) and disability (ie the meaning society attaches to the presence of impairment)' (Chappell et al, 2001, p.29). Disability is constructed in relation to the social, economic and political features of a society 'at a particular historical point' (p.29). The premise is that people with impairments can have satisfying lives as disabled people if the focus is shifted from *rehabilitating* them to fit into an unjust and unequal society, to removing the barriers that disable them (Finklestein and Stuart, 1996).

The social model is rights based and espouses equal citizenship, emancipation and inclusion. Rather than 'changing' disabled people to fit an unjust society, it is the systems, structures and institutions of society which need to change to reflect the diversity within the human race. Reinders (2002) says, 'The key notion ... is that of individual rights. It has often been remarked that what used to be a matter of charity is now a matter of rights. Social responsibility is not a matter of good will but of justice' (p.1).

It is, though, one thing to have a conceptual model which seeks to explain how learning disability is socially constructed, and another to see this expressed in action. From the concept, and closely linked to it, has arisen the disability rights movement and demands for social inclusion, both of which have significance for people with learning disabilities.

The social model of disability and people with learning disabilities

There has been much debate recently about the implications of the social model of disability for people with learning disabilities. To some extent people with learning disabilities have been ignored by the disability movement and their experiences largely negated. Goodley (2004) writes, 'The British engagement with the social model, with its roots in organisations of disabled people with physical and sensory impairments ... has often created a view of learning difficulties as an unproblematic biological impairment' (p.49) and contends that the activism of people with learning disabilities, particularly through the self-advocacy movement, has not been given the serious recognition accorded to the wider movement of disabled people. This has been denied on the grounds that the model grew out of the experiences of people with physical impairments who were writing about their own lives, but also that the social model is intended to apply to all disabled people.

Campbell (1997) acknowledges the problems of the place of people with learning disabilities in the wider disability movement, saying, 'The greatest and perhaps hardest challenges to be faced are the alliances that need to be made with other oppressed groups, other civil rights activists and impairment groups within our movement who do not feel a part of the common struggle' (p.87).

In many ways, we could say that the social model of disability reflects the experiences of people with learning disabilities even more accurately than those of other groups. Take Goodey's (2003) contention, for example, 'that the notion of ID (intellectual disability) changes much quicker than the notion of physical disability largely because the notion of intelligence has been shown to be tailored following cultural interests. Whereas physical disability is the product of a 'built environment', ID is the product of cultural norms about what counts as human. In other words, more than anything else the notion of ID reflects how we think about ourselves as human beings' (Reinders, 2003, p.504).

Advantages and disadvantages of knowing the causes and effects of learning disability

One of the legacies of the medical model of disability is the extent of the knowledge about the causes of different types of learning disabilities and their effects. Whether or not this is a good thing is a much debated issue. Ho (2004) identifies several reasons why a diagnosis of learning disability might be useful for teachers, school officials and parents, but also raises questions. On the one hand, she says, a diagnosis establishes eligibility for certain types of support. On the other, it can provide an excuse for educators and legislators to adopt a medical approach and ignore problems within the educational and social systems that contribute to learning difficulties.

Knowing the cause of a particular learning disability can also be useful for ensuring appropriate health support, eg understanding the possibility of heart defects, sight or hearing impairment, respiratory and atlantoaxial instability (misalignment of the top two vertebrae of the neck) in people with Down syndrome.

There is also an argument that the more we know about a person's learning disability, the better we can design support systems, especially since some syndromes and conditions may be associated with particular difficulties, eg difficulties in communication and relationships as experienced by people with autistic spectrum disorders.

Knowing the cause of their son or daughter's learning disability can be helpful for parents. They can get further information about how the syndrome or condition is likely to affect their child and the possible implications for the family. They can meet other parents who have children with the same condition or syndrome and join self-help groups, establishing a collective voice to obtain their rights and the appropriate support. People with learning disabilities can also find it helpful to know the cause of their disability, find out more about it and help inform other people's knowledge through training and research, among other things. They have a right to know about their own syndrome or condition if they wish and to understand more about themselves. This knowledge can also help towards a collective identity and can enable them to fight against attempts to terminate pregnancies when a child has a particular condition, or to challenge health inequalities.

However, the disadvantages of knowing cause and possible effect outweigh the advantages. These include:

- the stigmatisation of people with learning disabilities

- stereotyping and expectations based on stereotyping

- the 'vicious circle' of low expectations, constrained opportunity which results in low achievement because of the denied opportunity

- exclusion and marginalisation

- the denial of our common humanity

- that it is contrary to social justice and equality

Another danger, not so much of knowing the causes and effects of a learning disability, but of categorising people at all, is that it leads to value judgements about people's lives. Quality of life has a largely subjective component – what right have I to decide whether or not someone else's life is worth living? Klotz (2004), in a discussion about understanding the lives of people with profound and multiple learning disabilities, points out that our focus on labels, constructs, structures and meanings does not allow us to 'actually enter into intellectually disabled people's worlds and relate to them as people who are already fully human and encultured' (p.101). She gives as an example Gleason's (1994) work with two multiply-disabled boys with no speech who interacted with one another and engaged in meaningful and intentional behaviour and whose apparently 'erratic and meaningless movement were ... purposeful and predictive' (p.101). (Something that won't surprise any of us who work with people with profound and multiple disabilities.)

One of the most controversial debates at present is that of genetics and prevention, which contains within it some elements of the old eugenics movement. This can be seen as a direct threat to the future existence of many disabled people. Among the issues are:

- the termination of pregnancy when a foetus is likely to have an impairment and who has the right to decide (Ward, 2001)

- genetic screening and who decides what is and isn't 'a good life' (Edwards, 2003)

- the perception of people with impairments as 'inferior' (Clapton, 2003)

- the significance of genetic screening for disabled people today (Stainton, 2003) and other people's perceptions of their 'quality of life'

There exists a wide range of views on these issues, as can be seen and heard when they periodically emerge in the media. The word 'eugenics' is seldom heard in these debates but the concept is still a live one.

Eugenics

The idea of eugenics had its roots in selective breeding of animals to improve the stock. It gained some strength from certain interpretations of Charles Darwin's theories on survival of the fittest of the species. These ideas were seen as applicable to humans and as a way of improving the quality of the human race.

As mentioned earlier in this book, positive eugenics was the proposal that groups of individuals seen as superior should be encouraged to have families. Negative eugenics was based on preventing people perceived as inferior from having children, the main tool for this being sterilisation. It can be seen where the latter concept in particular might lead with regard to people with learning disabilities.

Currently, largely because of advances in genetics, the focus has moved away from who should reproduce to who should be allowed to be born (Ward 2001).

Holland and Clare (2003) explore the conflict between the 'apparent benefits' of advances in gene technology for the population in general and the negative effects for people with learning disabilities and conclude:

- the principles of human rights are for everyone and cannot be withdrawn on the grounds of disability

- we should be extremely cautious about compromising individual rights for the benefit of society

- 'there is an urgent need for politicians and the public to devise explicit, and transparent, guidance which respects basic human rights' (p.524)

Support services and the social model of disability

The social model of disability, with its philosophy of social inclusion, has clear implications for today's support services. Thus the hallmarks of a service with social inclusion as its goal, as discussed in chapter 3, are similar to those of a service based on the social model of disability. These, you may remember, include openness, the use of ordinary resources and facilities, good community networks, being not only *in* the community but also *of* the community.

Such a service also espouses person centred principles and practices – individuality, diversity, the use of natural networks, taking the lead from the person, shared learning and support to achieve personal aspirations and a better life.

A service based on the social model of disability must also:

- recognise the injustices within society and be fully conversant with the barriers to social inclusion of people with learning disabilities

- work actively to combat prejudice and discrimination, both within the service and in the wider context

- take service users' experiences and opinions seriously

- involve service users (and, where relevant, families and advocates) in all aspects of planning, providing, monitoring and evaluating the service

- support service users in achieving and upholding their rights through individual representation, involvement in self-advocacy groups and the use of systems such as complaints procedures

- help build service users' capacity in a wide variety of ways so that they can express themselves in their preferred ways, make decisions and take control of their own lives

To what extent is your service based on the social model of disability? Think about this by doing the next activity.

ACTIVITY 9: **Your service and the social model**

Spend a bit of time reflecting on what you have learned about the social model of disability and thinking about how your service operates.

Now select some policy documents at random and read through them.

What do your reflections and these documents tell you about your service in relation to the social model of disability?

What do they tell you about the role of and the degree of priority given to the medical model in your service?

Are there any changes you would like to make?

Comment

Your service might be quite clearly based on the social model of disability or it might be a bit of a mixture. You might have considered physical barriers, informational barriers and barriers which separate workers and service users. Or the barriers might be more subtle. Being a community-based service (supported living, for instance) but working restricted hours or staff making the decisions, for example, or getting stuck in routines that prevent people building their capacities by trying new things. Or assuming because things are going well that people are quite happy with the current situation. Everyone gets stale – even services that were once the most progressive. Is it time for a rethink and, if so, what's your role and who else will be involved?

From *Valuing People*

People with learning disabilities should be fully involved in the decision-making processes that affect their lives. This applies to decisions on day-to-day matters such as choices of activities, operational matters such as staff selection and strategic matters such as changes to eligibility criteria. It is no longer acceptable for organisations to view people with learning disabilities as passive recipients of services; they must instead be seen as active partners (DoH, p.51).

Concluding comment

We've come a long way since the politics of eugenics and institutionalisation, but not nearly far enough, with some people still living in institutions and many others still leading excluded lives. The social model of disability holds great promise for people with learning disabilities if we pursue it with commitment and energy. In the words of Goodley (2004): 'too often, people with learning disabilities are only partially included in major theoretical developments in disability studies; their activism is not given the same weight as that of their physically impaired comrades; the leaders of the People First movement are too easily ignored and the policies and practices that impact upon their lives remain in the hands of the non-disabled policy-makers who created them' (p.49).

It's up to you and me to see that this changes. I've touched upon ways of doing this at various places throughout this book. Another is through better networks and partnership working, which is the focus of the final chapter.

Chapter 6

Networking

Introduction

The world is getting smaller. For good or ill, television brings us pictures of events as they occur, distance travel is becoming faster and available to increasing numbers of people and there is the growth of the global economy. Few countries or organisations operate in isolation. There are networks for all sorts of purposes.

This chapter is about networking, a key aspect of which I see as active collaboration which makes change possible. Additional aspects are illustrated below.

'Networking is a dynamic process involving people prepared to communicate and share with each other' (Hughes, 1999).

'Networking is a way of establishing and using contacts for information, support and other assistance' (Benton, 1997).

Valuing People in England and *The same as you?* in Scotland propose strategies for change unlike any we have previously encountered in the history of learning disability. They are especially significant because they are proactive. Fryson and Simons (2003) point out that the *Valuing People* White Paper represents a radical development in that it sets out the first *national* agenda for the future of services for people with learning disabilities for 30 years. The very idea of a 'national strategy' for learning disability represents a significant break with the recent past.

Both of these strategies rely heavily on networks. Their information and vision were derived from networks of people with a vested interest in making things better. Their implementation is being made possible by networking at local, regional and national level. Their ideas are influenced by networking with other nations and funding obtained through networks at different levels.

My exploration of networking includes the following issues:

- the role of networks in the development of support services

- why networks are important

- networking in relation to training, funding and advocacy

- the skills of networking

The role of networks in the development of support services

The changes envisioned in *Valuing People* and *The same as you?* are to be achieved through a series of interconnected networks.

The implementation of *Valuing People* is being done through a number of initiatives which involve networking.

These include a number of formal arrangements:

- *Learning Disability Partnership Boards (LDPBs)*, based on local authority areas and built on established inter-agency structures, which are responsible for achieving the objectives of *Valuing People*, services for adults and for overseeing inter-agency planning and commissioning of comprehensive and inclusive services which provide real options to people in their local community

- *Local Strategic Partnerships* for services for children

- *Joint Investment Plans* programmes involving local service providers in improving support on offer to specific groups such as people with learning disabilities

- *Integrated Professional Working*, as part of a review of Community Learning Disability Teams to see how well specialist professionals are working together

- *National Learning Disability Task Force* to 'monitor and support implementation by acting as a champion for change at local level' (DoH, 2001, p.111)

- *National Forum* to enable service users to participate in decision making and planning

Together with other networking approaches:

- funding which requires integrated approaches, eg the Learning Disability Development Fund and the Implementation Support Fund

- integrated information gathering and research

Similarly, *The same as you?* is being implemented through a variety of specific networking arrangements:

- *Partnership in Practice (PIP)* agreements formulated by local authorities, health boards and primary care trusts which form part of other networks such as those for community care, children's services and local health care co-operative plans

- *Local Area Co-ordinators* who work with individual people and their families on a local basis to help improve local services and get people the lives they want

- *The Scottish Consortium for Learning Disability (SCLD)*, a network of agencies which has established local networks throughout the country to take the vision forward (including the National Network for people with profound and multiple learning disabilities)

- *The Change Fund* and other funding linked to PIPs

- *Users and Carers Reference Group* to represent the views of service users and family carers and help take the strategy forward

All of these initiatives require the full and active participation of people with learning disabilities and their families. Fyson and Simons (2003) point out: 'In a significant departure from usual policy-making processes, *Valuing People* explicitly aimed to involve all relevant stakeholders during both its creation and its implementation' (p.153).

As a result of their findings from the 'Strategies for Change' project, funded by the Department of Health and designed to assess the progress of *Valuing People*, Fyson and Simons emphasise that:

- national strategy must be translated into local action, which will require effective local planning and effective local leadership

- all stakeholders must be involved, especially those with learning disabilities and their families

- much remains to be done, although many LDPBs are working hard to ensure meaningful involvement of people with learning disabilities

Clearly, networking is one of the key issues here.

Informal networks

These should not be forgotten in all the attention paid to formal networks. Family, friends, neighbours and the wider community can contribute and work in collaboration with each other and professionals. Activities such as various forms of advocacy and befriending actively work to build co-operative links between all types of network, formal and informal.

The benefits of networks

Our traditional way of working has been to rely on the 'experts' – the professionals – to lead the way in policy-making and service provision, leaving them to guard professional boundaries and identities and to work largely in isolation one from the other. The overall national learning disability strategies in the UK, as well as the policy initiatives which have resulted from them, are trying to break down these separatist barriers. This is not to say that there haven't been multidisciplinary initiatives before. But in few of them have people with learning disabilities or their families and advocates been true participants and partners, and this has diminished their value in networking and other ways.

In *Valuing People*, the DoH gives several reasons why partnership working is not widespread:

- lack of agreement about values and service objectives

- lack of agreement on financial arrangements

- the low priority given to joint working within organisations

In many ways it's much easier to work alone – real networking takes time and effort and presents challenges, especially if the people in the network have very different ideas from your own. In many ways networking, like other aspects of partnership working, remains more of an art than a science (Cameron, 2001).

But networking brings substantial benefits. For instance:

New ideas and challenges

We can easily become stuck in our own ways of doing things, fail to keep up to date or to see the flaws. Exposure to new ideas and practices can counteract this and prevent insularity.

A problem shared...

While a team approach takes longer it is more productive. Local people with local knowledge can cast a different kind of light on problems. People come at things from different angles. The perspectives of service users and carers can turn issues on their head and help others to see them differently. Different types of expertise can fill gaps.

Making and using connections

Networks facilitate information, skills and resource sharing and help members make new connections. In this way, links are made between different networks which enrich everyone involved.

ACTIVITY 10: **The benefits of networking**

The above are only some of the benefits of networking. You will be able to think of others. For this activity, identify one network to which you as a manager or senior worker belong and which may or may not include service users. Identify another to which only service users belong. List some of the benefits of each.

Your network
Describe the network
List the benefits

Service users' network
Describe the network
List the benefits

Describe ways in which these two networks benefited one another.

Comment

You might have identified the following benefits:

- seeing how different perspectives compared

- changing aspects of the service as a result of these different perspectives

- gaining new insights

- finding new ways of involving service users

- forming new alliances

- obtaining additional resources

- making information more accessible

Which others did you include?

Networking in relation to training, funding and advocacy

Three areas that can benefit particularly from being involved in regional networks are training, funding and advocacy.

Networking and training

There's a tendency to think of paid employees when we discuss training. The much wider vision of our national strategies means we must include service users and family carers in training plans – not only in undergoing training, but also in providing training. Some organisations already do this, of course. For example, Key Housing, a Scottish agency and partner member of the Scottish Consortium for Learning Disability (SCLD), has for many years trained people with learning disabilities as trainers of staff. The SCLD itself has an unequivocal policy of having a co-trainer with a learning disability on all its training courses and events, and provides ongoing training to support people in doing this. You can find out more by logging on to the SCLD website (www.scld.org.uk). The British Institute of Learning Disabilities is similarly preparing people with learning disabilities to work as training associates.

The Learning Disabilities Awards Framework (LDAF) has been established to improve the skills and qualifications of the workforce in England, Wales and Northern Ireland. Funding for training is available through government schemes. In Scotland, the SCLD has a prime role in training linked to the Scottish strategy. All stakeholders are involved in the planning and design of training programmes and events.

Networking also provides opportunities for agencies to make use of one another's training events. It is quite common now for smaller agencies to be part of training networks and access training which might otherwise not be available. Larger organisations are increasingly opening up their training to others, including service users and family trainers. Networking cuts across traditional training boundaries, so training need no longer remain under the 'learning disability' banner but become more inclusive. True, we need to retain specialist

'learning disability' training for some things, but not for others. Why shouldn't people with learning disabilities access the same small business training and opportunities as other people, for example, or the same catering courses?
The advantages are not one sided. 'Mainstream' organisations benefit by becoming more inclusive and making information and training methods more accessible.

Networking and funding

Partnership working is a requirement of the funding strategies of *Valuing People* and *The same as you?* Services won't have access unless they are part of regional networks. Other funding initiatives, such as the European Social Fund (ESF) require collaboration between networks of people. Many charitable private-sector funding initiatives either require evidence of networking and partnership working or are favourably influenced by it in considering applications. Networking also brings other opportunities, enabling services to diversify their sources and avoid overreliance on one funder.

You might like to read. . .

Resourcing the Vision – Funding Valuing People by Paradigm (2003) which you can access on www.valuingpeople.gov.uk/documents/Resourcingthevision/pdf

---

Regional networks also enable access to things such as direct payments.

Networking and advocacy

The new vision requires much stronger voices for people with learning disabilities, with advocacy as one of the key features. Recommendation 11 in *The same as you?* is: 'The Scottish Executive should continue to encourage the development of local independent advocacy services' (p.36). Objective 3 in *Valuing People* reads: 'To enable people with learning disabilities to have as much choice and control as possible over their lives through advocacy and a person centred approach to planning the services they need' (p.124). To achieve this, the DoH (England) and the Welsh Assembly Government have increased funding for all forms of advocacy through the Advocacy Grant Schemes.

You might like to read. . .

Information about the National Coalition of Citizen Advocacy Schemes
can be found by logging on to www.bild.cacoalition.org.uk

Information about the Advocacy Federation can be found by logging on
to the Advocacy Resource Exchange (formerly known as CAIT) at
www.citizenadvocacy.org.uk

Information about the Advocacy Alliance can be found by logging on to www.nas.org.uk

Information about strengthening self-advocacy infrastructures
can be found by logging on to www.via.org

Networking is the cornerstone of advocacy. It contributes to the collective voice
with people with learning disabilities and facilitates the dissemination of ideas,
experiences and information. Perhaps most importantly of all it raises the status
of people with learning disabilities and helps them move towards their stated aim
– positive recognition, respect and control over their own lives.

Networking for change

In short, networking is essential to change. Without it change will still happen,
but in a much more limited way and possibly not in the right direction. However
skilled and knowledgeable any individual or organisation, there is no substitute
for exposure to new ideas. Jukes (2003) says: 'Managing change is not only
confined to individual practitioners and singular services, but is also perceived
as a multidisciplinary and agency activity, and those practitioners responsible for
change must possess or have access to a wide range of skills, resources, support
and knowledge, in order to activate the change process' (p. 572).

Writing about the role of specialist learning disability services, Jenkins et al (2003)
say: 'the nature of such services has changed over time and that currently further
changes are being proposed. The challenge in coming years is to develop specialist
services that enhance independence and well-being whilst promoting the inclusion
of people with learning disabilities in both generic services and wider society. This
demands that professionals working within specialist services work collaboratively
and that they use their skills and expertise in a flexible manner' (p.364).

The skills of networking

Jukes (2003) identifies two crucial roles for managers: those of change agent and of leader. Leadership does not negate or undermine networking, but makes it workable. Some of the skills and capacity required for these roles include:

- a clear understanding of the vision

- good local connections with links to other networks, local, regional, national and international

- a clear and up-to-date knowledge of the national strategy for learning disability

- an ability to reflect on and improve your own communication and interpersonal skills

- the ability to inspire and motivate people and to support them in working towards the vision

- negotiation and conflict resolution

- planning

- flexibility

This list could go on and on, but I'll stop there. You will be able to add to it from your own experience.

ACTIVITY 11: **Networking skills and capacities**

Read through the list above. Select three things you are particularly good at and list them here.

Now describe how each skill or capacity has enabled you to advance networking in relation to your own service with particular reference to how it facilitated fuller participation for service users in some aspect of your service.

Finally, briefly describe three benefits to the service as a whole which derive from being part of local and regional networks and working in partnership with other agencies, people with learning disabilities and family carers.

Comment

I thought of the following three benefits:

- finding new connections and alliances with people involved in similar developments within their service

- being able to access new sources of funding

- getting better ideas of what families feel about support services and how they should develop in the future

Were your answers similar to mine in any way or completely different? Which other benefits did you identify?

Concluding comment

One of the primary purposes of networking is to accelerate change. Change brings together all of the issues discussed throughout the book and points us towards the future – a better future, we hope, for people with learning disabilities and their families. A future which will bring us closer to an inclusive society where all people with learning disabilities play their part and are accorded their full rights. Where we might be able to stop calling them 'people with learning disabilities' but just know them as people, like everyone else. That's a long way off, I know, but it will come. People with learning disabilities and their families are at the centre of this process of change by right; many of the rest of us are there because we're paid to be. Networking provides all of us with the opportunity to put our heads, ideas, experiences and talents together to make change happen as quickly as possible. We have a commitment and a responsibility to do this.

References

Arthur, A. (2003) 'The emotional lives of people with learning disability' *British Journal of Learning Disabilities*, 31, 25–30

Atherton, H. (2003) 'A history of learning disabilities' in Gates, B. (ed) *Learning Disabilities: Towards Inclusion* Edinburgh: Churchill Livingstone

Barnes, C. (1997) 'A Legacy of Oppression: A History of Disability in Western Culture' in Barton, L. and Oliver, M. (eds) *Disability Studies: Past, Present and Future* Leeds: The Disability Press

Barron, D. (2000) 'From community to institution – and back again' in Brigham, L., Atkinson, D., Jackson, M., Rolph, S. and Walmsley, J. (eds) *Crossing Boundaries* Kidderminster: British Institute of Learning Disabilities

Benton, D. C. (1997) 'Networking' *Nursing Standard* 35, 47–52

Bersani, H. Jr (1998) 'From Social Clubs to Social Movement: Landmarks in the development of the international self-advocacy movement' in Ward, L. (ed) *Innovations in Advocacy and Empowerment for People with Intellectual Disabilities* Chorley, Lancashire: Lisieux Hall

Borland, J. and Ramcharan, P. (1997) 'Part 1 Conclusion. Empowerment in Informal Settings' in Ramcharan, P., Roberts, G., Grant, G. and Borland, J. (eds) *Empowerment in Everyday Life. Learning Disability*. London: Jessica Kingsley

Bradshaw, J. (2001) 'Complexity of staff communication and reported level of understanding skills in adults with intellectual disability' *Journal of Intellectual Disability Research* 45, 3, 233–243

Brigham, L. (2000) 'Understanding segregation from the nineteenth to the twentieth century: redrawing boundaries and the problem of pollution' in Brigham, L., Atkinson, D., Jackson, M., Rolph, S. and Walmsley, J. (eds) *Crossing Boundaries* Kidderminster: British Institute of Learning Disabilities

Brigham, L., Atkinson, D., Jackson, M., Rolph, S. and Walmsley, J. (eds) (1997) *Crossing Boundaries* Kidderminster: British Institute of Learning Disabilities

Cameron, A. (2001) *The Art of Partnership: A Practical Guide* Kidderminster: British Institute of Learning Disabilities

Campbell, J. (1997) 'Growing Pains' Disability Politics – The journey explained and described in Barton, L. and Oliver, M. (eds) *Disability Studies: Past, Present and Future* Leeds: The Disability Press

Chappell, A. L. (2000) 'Emergence of participatory methodology in learning difficulty research: understanding the context' *British Journal of Learning Disabilities* 28, 38–43

Chappell, A. L., Goodley, D. and Lawthom, R. (2001) 'Making connections: the relevance of the social model of disability for people with learning difficulties' *British Journal of Learning Disabilities* 29, 45–50

Clapton, J. (2003) 'Tragedy and catastrophe: contentious discourses of ethics and disability' *Journal of Intellectual Disability Research*, 47, 7, 540–547

DoH (Department of Health) (2001) *Valuing People: A New Strategy for Learning Disability for the 21st Century* London: Department of Health

Downer, J. and Ferns, P. (1993) 'Self Advocacy By Black People With Learning Difficulties' in Beresford, P. and Harding, T (Eds), *A Challenge To Change: Practical experiences of building user-led services*, London: National Institute for Social Work

Edwards, S. D. (2003) 'Prenatal screening for intellectual disability' *Journal of Intellectual Disability Research*, 47, 7, 526–532

Felce, D., Grant, G., Todd, S., Ramcharan, P., Beyer, S., McGrath, M., Perry, J., Shearn, J., Kilsby, M. and Lowe, K. (1998) *Towards a full life: researching policy innovation for people with learning disabilities* Oxford: Butterworth Heinemann

Fido, R. and Potts, P. (1997) 'Using Oral Histories' in Atkinson, D., Jackson, M. and Walmsley, J. (eds) *Forgotten lives: Exploring the History of Learning Disability* Kidderminster: British Institute of Learning Disabilities

Finklestein, V. and Stuart, O. (1996) 'Developing New Services' in Hales, G. (1996) (ed) *Beyond Disability – Towards an Enabling Society* London: Sage

Fyson, R. and Simons, K. (2003) 'Strategies for change: making *Valuing People* a reality'. *British Journal of Learning Disabilities* 31, 153–158

Gates, B. and Wilberforce, D. (2003) 'The nature of learning disabilities' in Gates, B. (ed) *Learning Disabilities: Towards Inclusion* Edinburgh: Churchill Livingstone

Goodey, C. F. (2003) 'On certainty, reflexivity and the ethics of genetic research into intellectual disability' *Journal of Intellectual Disability Research*, 47, 7, 501–504

Goodley, D. (2004) Editorial, *British Journal of Learning Disabilities* 32, 49–51

Grant, G. (1997) 'Consulting to Involve or Consulting to Empower?' in Ramcharan, P., Roberts, G., Grant, G. and Borland, J. (eds) *Empowerment in Everyday Life: Learning Disability* London: Jessica Kingsley

Ho, A. (2004) 'To be labelled or not to be labelled: that is the question' *British Journal of Learning Disabilities* 32, 86–92

Holland, A. and Clare, I. C. H. (2003) 'The Human Genome Project: considerations for people with intellectual disabilities' *Journal of Intellectual Disability Research* 47, 7, 515–525

Hughes, M. (1999) 'The Missing Link' *Nursing Times* 95, 5

Hunt, P. (1966) 'A Critical Condition' in Hunt, P. (ed) *Stigma: The Experience of Disability* London: Geoffrey Chapman

Jenkins, R., Mansell, I. and Northway, R. (2003) 'Specialist learning disability services in the UK' in Gates, B. (ed) *Learning Disabilities. Towards Inclusion* Edinburgh: Churchill Livingstone

Jukes, M. (2003) 'Management and leadership in learning disabilities' in Gates, B. (ed) *Learning Disabilities: Towards Inclusion* Edinburgh: Churchill Livingstone

Kevan, F. (2003) 'Challenging behaviour and communication difficulties' *British Journal of Learning Disabilities*, 31, 75–80

King's Fund (1980) *An Ordinary Life* London: Kings Fund

Klotz, J. (2004) 'Sociocultural study of learning disability: moving beyond labelling and social constructionist perspective' *British Journal of Learning Disabilities* 32, 93–104.

Knapp, M., Cambridge, P., Thomason, C., Beecham, J., Allen, C. and Darton, R. (1992) *Care in the Community: Challenge and Demonstration* Aldershot: Ashgate

Lancioni, G. E. et al (2002) 'Evaluating the use of multiple microswitches and responses for children with multiple disabilities' *Journal of Intellectual Disability Research* 46, 4, 346-351

Maudslay, L. et al (2003) *Aasha: working with young people with a learning difficulty from a South Asian background* London: SKILL

McConkey, R., Purcell, M. and Morris, I. (1999) 'Staff perceptions of communication with a partner who is intellectually disabled' *Journal of Applied Research in Intellectual Disabilities* 12, 204–210

McNally, S. (2003) 'Helping to empower people' in Gates, B. (ed) *Learning Disabilities: Towards Inclusion* Edinburgh: Churchill Livingstone

Means, R. and Smith, R. (1994) *Community Care: Policy and Practice*, 2nd edition, London: Macmillan

Mitchell, D. (2000) 'Ambiguous boundaries: retrieving the history of learning disability nursing' in Brigham, L., Atkinson, D., Jackson, M., Rolph, S. and Walmsley, J. (eds) *Crossing Boundaries* Kidderminster: British Institute of Learning Disabilities

Mount, B. (1990) *Making Futures Happen: a manual for facilitators of personal futures planning* Governor's Council on Developmental Disabilities, Minnesota

Nirje, B. (1980) 'The normalisation principle' in Flynn, R. J. and Nitsch, K. E. (eds) *Normalisation, Social Integration and Community Services* Baltimore: University Park Press

O'Brien, J. and Tyne, A. (1981) *The Principle of normalisation: a foundation for effective services* London: Values into Action

Oliver, M. (1983) *Social Work with Disabled People* Basingstoke: Macmillan

Oliver, M. (1996) *Understanding Disability: From Theory to Practice* London: Macmillan

Oswin, M. (1971) *The Empty Hours* London: The Penguin Press

Oswin, M. (2000) 'Revisiting The Empty Hours' in Brigham, L., Atkinson, D., Jackson, M., Rolph, S. and Walmsley, J. (eds) *Crossing Boundaries* Kidderminster: British Institute of Learning Disabilities

Patton, M. (1990) *Qualitative Evaluation Methods*, 2nd edition, Beverly Hills, CA: Sage

Pearpoint, J., O'Brien, J. and Forest, M. (1993) *PATH: A Workbook for Planning Positive Possible Futures* Toronto: Inclusion Press

Ramcharan, P. and Borland, J. (1997) 'Preface' in Ramcharan, P., Roberts, G., Grant, G. and Borland, J. (eds) *Empowerment in Everyday Life: Learning Disability* London: Jessica Kingsley

Reinders, H. S. (2002) 'The good life for citizens with intellectual disability' *Journal of Intellectual Disability Research 46*, 1, 1–5

Reinders, H. S. (2003) 'Introduction to intellectual disability, genetics and ethics' *Journal of Intellectual Disability Research 47*, 7, 501–504

Rioux, M. (1997) 'When Myths Masquerade as Science: Disability Research from an Equality–Rights Perspective' in Barton, L. and Oliver, M. (eds) *Disability Studies: Past, Present and Future* Leeds: The Disability Press

Sanderson, H. (2000) 'Person Centred Planning: Key Features and Approaches' available from www.paradigm-uk.org

Sanderson, H. (2003) 'Person centred planning' in Gates, B. (ed) *Learning Disabilities: Towards Inclusion* Edinburgh: Churchill Livingstone

Sanderson, H., Kennedy, J., Ritchie, P. and Goodwin, G. (2002) *People, Plans and Possibilities – Exploring Person Centred Planning* Edinburgh: Scottish Human Services

Scottish Executive (2000) *The same as you? A review of services for people with learning disabilities* Edinburgh: The Scottish Executive

Souza, A. with Ramcharan, P. (1997) 'Everything You Ever Wanted to Know About Down's Syndrome, but Never Bothered to Ask' in Ramcharan, P., Roberts, G., Grant, G. and Borland, J. (eds) *Empowerment in Everyday Life: Learning Disability* London: Jessica Kingsley

Stainton, T. (2000) 'Equal citizens? The discourse of liberty and rights in the history of learning disabilities' in Brigham, L., Atkinson, D., Jackson, M., Rolph, S. and Walmsley, J. (eds) *Crossing Boundaries* Kidderminster: British Institute of Learning Disabilities

Stainton, T. (2003) 'Identity, difference and the ethical politics of prenatal testing' *Journal of Intellectual Disability Research*, 47, 7, 533–539

Styring, L. (2003) 'Community care: opportunities, challenges and dilemmas' in Markwick, A. and Parrish, A. (eds) *Learning Disabilities: Themes and Perspectives* Edinburgh: Butterworth Heinemann

Sweeney, C. and Sanderson, H. (February 2002) *Person Centred Planning: BILD Factsheet* Kidderminster: British Institute of Learning Disabilities

Vlachou, A.D. (1997) *Struggles for Inclusive Education* Buckingham: Open University Press

Walmsley, J. (1997) 'Telling the History of Learning Disability from Local Sources' in Atkinson, D., Jackson, M. and Walmsley, J. (eds) *Forgotten lives: Exploring the History of Learning Disability* Kidderminster: British Institute of Learning Disabilities

Walmsley, J. and Downer, J. (1997) 'Shouting the Loudest: Self-Advocacy, Power and Diversity' in Ramcharan, P., Roberts, G., Grant, G. and Borland, J. (eds) *Empowerment in Everyday Life: Learning Disability* London: Jessica Kingsley

Walsh, P. N. (1997) 'One world-new territory: European perspectives on intellectual disability' *Journal of Intellectual Disability Research* 41, 2, 112–119

Warburg, M. (2001) 'Visual impairment in adult people with intellectual disability: Literature review' *Journal of Intellectual Disability Research* 45, 5, 424–438

Ward, L . (2001) *Considered Choices? The new genetics, prenatal testing and people with learning disabilities* Kidderminster: British Institute of Learning Disabilities

Ward, L. (ed) (1998) *Innovations in Advocacy and Empowerment for People with Intellectual Disabilities* Chorley: Lisieux Publications

Wolfensberger, W. and Tullman, S. (2002) 'The principle of normalisation' in Bytheway, B., Bacigalupo, V., Bornat, J., Johnson, J. and Spurr, S. *Understanding care, welfare and community: A reader* London: Routledge and The Open University

Resources

Websites

Association for Real Change (previously
Association for Residential Care)

www.arcuk.org.uk

British Institute of Learning Disabilities

www.bild.org.uk

Department of Health

www.doh.gov.uk/learningdisabilities

Disability Rights Commission

www.drc-gb.org

Mencap

www.mencap.org.uk

Norah Fry Research Centre

www.bris.ac.uk/Depts/NorahFry

People First

www.peoplefirst.org.uk

Scottish Consortium for Learning Disability

www.scld.co.uk

Scottish Executive

www.scotland.gov.uk/ldsr

Scottish Human Services Ltd

www.shstrust.org.uk

Welsh Assembly

www.wales.gov.uk

Useful publications

NB. In addition to the publications listed below,
you will also find many of the books in the reference
list useful.

Advocacy and self-advocacy

Brooke, J. (2001) *Good Practice in Citizen Advocacy*
Kidderminster: British Institute of Learning
Disabilities

Equal Say (undated) *A Beginner's Guide to Citizen
Advocacy* (A5 leaflet) www.equalsay.org

Choice and Empowerment

Capability Scotland (2003) *X Marks the Spot:
A Guide to Voting for Disabled People* available
from www.capability-scotland.org.uk

Edge, J. (2001) *Who's in Control? Decision making
by people with learning disabilities who have high
support needs* London: Values into Action

Enable (1999) *Use Your Vote – Get Ready for
Elections* available from www.enable.org.uk

Gramlich, S., McBride, G., Snelham, N. and
Myers, B. with Williams, V. and Simons, K.
(2002) *Journey to Independence: What self advocates
tell us about direct payments* Kidderminster:
British Institute of Learning Disabilities

Communication

Grove, N. (2000) *See What I Mean: Guidelines
to aid understanding of communication by people
with severe and profound learning disabilities*
Kidderminster: British Institute of Learning
Disabilities

Nind, M. and Hewett, D. (2000) *A Practical Guide
to Intensive Interaction* Kidderminster: British
Institute of Learning Disabilities

Culture and Ethnicity

DH (2001) *Learning Difficulties and Ethnicity*
London: Department of Health

DRC and CERES (April 2004) *Our Rights,
Our Choices: Meeting the information needs
of black and minority ethnic disabled people*
available from www.drc-gb.org

Housing

Dixon, T. (2001) *Shared Ownership for People
with Learning Disabilities* Kidderminster:
British Institute of Learning Disabilities

Harker, M. and King, T. (2002)
*Renting Your Own Home: Housing options for
people with learning disabilities* Kidderminster:
British Institute of Learning Disabilities

Inclusive education

Down's Syndrome Association and Scottish
Down's Syndrome Association (undated)
Including Pupils with Down's Syndrome available
from www.downs-syndrome.org.uk

SCLD (2003) *Top Marks for Good Practice –
Getting the Most for Your Child's Schooling*
available from www.scld.org.uk

Learning disability

Emerson, E, et al (2000) *Learning Disabilities:
the fundamental facts* London: The Foundation
for People with Learning Disabilities

Relationships and sexuality

Cambridge, P. (1996) *The Sexuality and Sexual
Rights of People with Learning Disabilities:
Considerations for Staff and Carers* Kidderminster:
British Institute of Learning Disabilities

McCarthy, M. and Cambridge, P. (1996)
Your Rights about Sex Kidderminster:
British Institute of Learning Disabilities